Manchester takes on the Olympic world at Monte Carlo

It was just 8am and we were on the streets at the gates of the Monte Carlo Sporting Club with the kids from the band, waving Union Jacks as the IOC delegates entered for day four of the one-hundred-and-first IOC Session. The torrential rain was to last through the day and night of September 23rd. 1993. It was, we all agreed, an omen. But which way?

One of the limousines slowed as it drew level with us and the rear window slid down. It was Princess Anne and she smiled at the kids with genuine warmth. The only other major presence at the Sporting Club gates was the Berliners. One particularly nutty German decided that he could compete with the kids' chanting of 'Manchester, Manchester,' but his good natured shouting for 'Berlin' was no competition to bubbling enthusiasm of the kids from Levenshulme in the rain. The time had come. We showered the Mediterranean rain away and donned our British Bid uniforms of blue blazers, grey trousers, white shirts, Bid ties and Panama hats before reconvening in the lobby of the hotel.

As I entered the lift on the sixth floor I was aware of six or seven people standing in silence facing me. I accompanied them in silence for a few seconds as I realised that they were all members of the Sydney Bid Team in their own corporate uniforms. The doors of the lift slid quietly shut behind me. There was a further silence as we surveyed each other apprehensively and then a voice from the back drawled, "Welcome to Austraaalia."

I didn't know it then, but it was a portent of things to come. But it's pretty much been part of the story of my life. Right place, not necessarily right time...

...but I'm getting ahead of myself, ooh, by about 40 years...

Manc

A few weeks ago a techie friend of mine (whilst trying to teach me, of the too-late generation about techie things) and I were talking about Manchester. I said to Paul that I'd love to do a book like Martin Stockley had, about his work in the City. Of course Paul said, "Just do it." And when I said I couldn't afford the big budget hardback of Martin's admirable efforts Paul said to me: "Haven't you learnt anything? Publish it on-line and it won't cost you anything." Being polemic as always I immediately countered with, "It would have to be designed well and you can't do that on-line," showing him a few examples of how on-line design looks crap. But then he'd created a web-site for my business (one of them) which didn't look crap and so I was proven wrong at the first hurdle.

Now this interested me, because (as I went on to tell Paul) I've got a cardboard box in my office in Manchester into which, for 30 years, I've been throwing photos (Boots processing…nobody looks at digital photographs do they?) and memorabilia. To be honest I've no idea what's at the bottom of the box because it's just filled up gradually for those years and I've never delved into it. Paul said, "Stick post-its onto a white wall and map the story you want to tell." But sod that, I've just started writing so I'll finish. If I need photos and memorabilia I'll match it all up afterwards. I'm curious now about what's actually at the bottom of that cardboard box.

So I'm mentally making a few notes as I start; actually I've been making these mental notes since Paul first mentioned this and, to be honest, they've not changed any. And they're not notes, just rules. I don't know exactly what I'm going to write but I know that I have to steer clear of my personal life, which has been complicated, to say the least. And I know that in some (maybe many cases) I'll have to change or omit names to protect the innocent – and the guilty.

But there are some – a couple no longer with us whom I either loved dearly or was very fond of – that I will have to name to put everything into context. I suspect that the last thing any 'author' does is to look again at his intro… and change it. But I hope that I don't change these few words, because they are from the heart.

Beginnings

I love my City. How anyone can not love a City I just don't know. It's not jingoistic and it's not unusual. Look at the Scousers – and what have they got to love? I don't know, but I also guess it's the same the world round. I wonder if anyone can love their city if they weren't born there, or at least grew up there? I've stayed here or hereabouts all my life. Areas around a city used to be called suburbs, or outlying areas, or all sorts of other things. Now we have 'Manchester City Region.' I'm not sure, but I think that somewhere along the line I might have been involved in creating that particular phrase. Anyway, I was born, I have worked and I still live in the Manchester City Region. And, as I say, I love my city.

I was born in 1953 in North Manchester and my earliest, earliest memory is of tipping my baby sister's pram up, out in our back garden in Blackley. I remember being horrified at what I had done and have vague recollections of my mum panicking. So I must have been around two, or a tad older, because my sister is two years younger than me. After that I have only mixed up memories of the usual kid things: playing in a street that is now no longer wide enough to take the cars parked either side – cars were few and far between then; riding on the back of the milk float before being spotted and chucked off. I walked home from that incident feeling embarrassed when as a Manc. I should have been proud of doing something cheeky.

And I vividly remember cutting my thumb badly on cup final day and my dad having to take me to hospital just before kick off. He must have been planning to listen on the radio, because we didn't get a telly until years later. He wasn't pleased, I know.

But there's another football memory, one that has stuck with me, maybe because even to a five year old it was eerie.

I remember walking along Corporation Street, near what is now the CIS building, having just got off the 53 bus from Blackley. I couldn't understand why it was so quiet and why everyone seemed to be standing around reading papers. It must have been February 7th. 1958, the day after the Munich air disaster. I wasn't aware of what had happened. I just have this memory of a weirdly silent city and people standing around with newspapers.

During the two to five year old period we moved to Middleton from Blackley and my parents worrying about paying £200 for a house. I remember this one because I went to the solicitors with them and overheard mention of this frightening amount of money.

I also remember my dad, who was a brickie by trade, suddenly not being around for six months, apart from at weekends. He was retraining to be a social worker. How dramatic and adventurous a move that was in the 1950's I only came to realise with hindsight and the passage of several decades. I suspect many people reading this wouldn't even know that there were social workers in the 50's.

When he qualified this meant a move over the border. (As the maestro Eric Cantona so eloquently put it: The M62 between Manchester and Leeds is like the darkness of the night.) Well it wasn't Leeds, but I grew up in Bradford... Leeds City Region.

A move back to North Manchester when I was 11 (dodging the 11+ exam, because I missed it in Bury and it had been abolished in Bradford), I was chucked straight into grammar school. Whether I would have made it if I had had to take the exam I will, of course, never know. But I think that I was the only kid there who hadn't passed.

So we'll skip on to the fifth form and careers evenings. I had always been 'good at art.' But then everybody's kid is 'good at art' whether they are or not. However, I had always wanted to be a doctor. Sadly, the early teenage years don't stack up well for informing yourself that you are not actually bright enough to do what you think you want to do for a career. I had designed a poster for the school debating society (of which for some unknown reason I was a member – possibly because I'm bolshie) and one of the teachers said to me, "Have you thought of becoming a commercial artist?"

Well, two points. Firstly I hadn't and secondly I doubt whether you have ever heard of the profession of 'Commercial Artist.' This metamorphosed through a couple of decades to designer and even more so in the following couple of decades to the heights – even – of 'brand consultant.' Which is maybe what I have become.

And so I was ushered past the grandiose careers evening tables for potential medical students and steered towards the more arty and much more interesting tables festooned with work and information from the art colleges. I guess, so to speak, the die was cast.

Now maybe I should have moved away from my City Region and broadened my horizons. But instead I stayed in the City Region and went to Bolton College of Art and Design. I have to say that I loved it from day one. As with every 16 year old suddenly released on the world as a mini adult I was treated as such.

And of course doing what I did enjoy every day, whilst learning, was a joy. I met some great characters in both the students – some of whom I am still in touch with – and the tutors – some of whom I am still in touch with and sadly, some of whom are no longer with us. Two in particular were inspirational from the start: Lonsdale Bonner (great name!) and Trevor Lofthouse had a passion for their subject which I have to this day and which still grows every day. I wish that I could indulge my passion for art more completely, although the way in which I still do this will be revealed later on in this ramble through my life.

I completed a one-year foundation course exploring painting, drawing, ceramics, textiles, sculpture. Oh how I wish that I could do that all again now. But the one module which seemed to fit with me was graphic design. It was on this foundation module that I first met Ken Adshead and Tony Forster.

Again, they were inspirational characters and Tony, who sadly died in 2008, became my friend, mentor and confidante for the rest of his life. I was privileged to be asked to give the eulogy at his funeral and again will write lots more about this remarkable man who saw himself as so unremarkable, but feel that including his eulogy here speaks volumes.

Fozzie

The Friday before last, instead of my usual two pages of rambling in my diary, I wrote: 'Fozzie died today. Teacher, friend, ally, confidante.

And so, if Tony's family here will allow me at this time, the first note in these words is that so many of us knew him just as Fozzie. And I guess that for those of us who called him Fozzie, the same words that I wrote in my diary sums up our relationship with this extraordinary man.

Fozzie will be cringing now as I use the word 'extraordinay.' But all of us here who recognise that sequence of words will understand, I am sure, why the word extraordinary is exactly right. So many of us here first met Fozzie as our teacher, than as a friend then an ally, then a trusted confidante. When I was talking to his son Dan last week about how we could let everyone – so many, many people – know about Fozzie's death, I flippantly suggested that he set up a web-site. Of course Dan didn't, but the domain name would have been easy to choose. The same as Fozzie's e-mail address: soddincomputers@yahoo.co.uk. Of course Fozzie would have liked a slightly different word than 'soddin' in his e-mail address. But this note also gives me the opportunity to replace a word in Fozzie's catch phrase that is a little more appropriate to use here at St. Stephen's.

So let's go back to almost the beginning and one of Fozzie's proudest mementos. We've all heard about it before, but for one last time I'll repeat it. His less than glowing school report that said, 'Wastes all his time drawing fancy letters.' Not such a waste of time as it turned out.

Like so many of us I had some extraordinary times with Fozzie and many years after he finished teaching me (although that never really ended) I was lucky enough to work with him for a number of years. Just one extraordinary time was dinner with Jeanne Larcher, Tony Dispigna, Ricardo Rousselot, Paula Scher and Seymour Chwast. Jeanne, Ricardo and Tony Dispigna began – as people who love letters do – to draw on the paper tablecloth. Yes, it was a classy joint! Fozzie watched them, until collectively they persuaded him to 'pen' some beautiful letters himself. He protested at first, of course, but they said, "You taught us how to do this."

I still have that paper table cloth.

And we all have Fozzie stories, all equally as good. But a couple will suffice to bring back your own memories of Fozzie times. Like the many times he crafted for hours on a piece of type and, when he showed it to me I said, "Fozzie, that's absolutely beautiful. But you don't spell it like that." To which he'd reply, of course, "Well sod me feller." Or something...similar. It wasn't that he couldn't spell, it was just that he only had eyes for the letters he loved. Actually, he wasn't that good at spelling...

Or the time that he was working on the logo for Manchester's Olympic Bid, a time when a young Daniel was picking up swimming medals for fun. Fozzie threw down his pencil and when I asked him what was up he said, "Sod me feller. I've just been thinking. My son's going to be swimming in the Olympics and just my luck. It'll be at Salford soddin' Quays."

So, Fozzie: medical mystery. We all worried for him, Polly, Simon and Daniel throughout every illness of the past. Almost 30 years. It seems that the only one that laughed through it all – at least outwardly – was Fozzie himself. I remember, it was in a pub and I think it was in Dublin. A perfect stranger, no doubt emboldened by Guinness, asked Fozzie what had happened to his face. Lupus was, of course, a boring answer to give. And so Fozzie attained hero status very quickly as he told how he had been serving on HMS Sheffield in the Falklands war when the missile hit.

Even his last re-writing of medical history, only finally cured last year by the only surgeon in the country capable of such an operation, was described by Fozzie as a boil on the bum. Some boil on the bum.

But through all this, anybody else, any one of us with a question, a concern, a problem, an illness. Well Fozzie didn't laugh he listened. So recently, as always, every single conversation between us – his friends – always included the two words, "How's Fozzie?" "Fine, in good form." And he was, right until the end. I hope Polly will forgive me for repeating this, but her last words to her husband were, "Tony, stop messing about." But this time of course, he wasn't.

Of course we all loved Fozzie. But of course a different kind of love to that he had for Polly, Simon – his precious grandchildren Lewis and Jack – and Daniel...and that they had for him. Everyone here today is testimony to that love. Friends and family. And I know that all of Fozzie's friends are here today for his family. So, Fozzie goes green. When Dan told me that his dad was being buried in a cardboard coffin I said that I hope it's a good stock. 1750 gram at least. Dan said he was going to put stickers on that said, 'Do Not Bend' and 'This Way Up.' Nicely designed stickers of course. In the end he settled for a sticker that just said, 'Return To Sender.' Fozzie is laughing along too.

Last words? It's so easy on these occasions to say how many friends the person had. But for me and perhaps above all else, what did make Fozzie extraordinary is that he made so many friends and not a single enemy.

In those days the equivalent of a degree course was four years; quite a stint with a one year foundation course at the start. My kids (the grown up ones) did sixth-form college for two years and then a three-year degree course (one of them a two year masters after that). That's the equivalent of five years at college, but it was still a long haul. There are so many stories from that time. And the worst proponents of silliness were the tutors. Inspirational AND daft. What a combination!

Tony Forster was the biggest joker and, it has to be said, would have been fired many times over in this politically correct world in which we now live. One of his typical stunts was asking (well endowed) teenage girls to deliver an envelope to another tutor in another building. When the young lady did so and the other tutor received the envelope he would read the message, 'Look at the tits on this!' Other stunts that I witnessed – and there were many – were such as us doing a photo-shoot for a poster involving a couple of five pound notes invisibly sellotaped onto the front of a roll of blank paper. Working late we resolved to go for a Chinese and a couple of beers. When the bill came Tony took out the roll and a pair of scissors which had been concealed about his person and, to the proprietor's confusion, cut off a couple of fivers from the roll and let them drop onto the tray with the bill.

When Frans Hals' Laughing Cavalier was stolen from a gallery, another tutor painted a facsimile using Ken Adshead's face (a remarkable likeness to the Cavalier himself) and was caught trying to hang it up in Manchester City Art Gallery. Banksy before Banksy was born.

And of course alcohol played its important part, but strangely more with the tutors than the students. I remember one tutor who turned up on his moped at a college fancy dress party dressed as a monk and sporting his own bottle of whisky. The problem was that he turned up on his moped and left on his moped with the bottle – now more than half empty – in the pocket of his habit. Disaster ensued, of course, and when the ambulance arrived, he was carted off to hospital. One or two members of staff were called by the hospital to collect him and deposit him back at his flat. They did so and left him tucked up unconscious, cut and bruised. When they called round the next morning to check on his welfare he woke up and said to them, "That was an awful party last night…who invited all those nurses?"

There were so many stories. My tutors all seemed so old and worldly and yet they were only 10 years or so older than me. It was a golden time at Bolton College of Art, thanks entirely to exceptional passion and talent amongst the tutors who managed to convey that passion to many students, me amongst them. This was particularly due to Tony Forster who was renowned worldwide for his typographic skills. Tony's passion was ultimately largely his undoing; after I left he became obsessive with his typographic work and the exceptional quality he produced led him to teach all day and then work through many nights in succession with no sleep. Illness overcame him after years of this and, although he never once complained, his life thereafter was plagued by these illnesses until the day he died.

When I left – in 1974 – I had my exit interview with the Head of the Graphic Design Department, Ken Adshead. Ken told me that I was a conundrum. "You could have been an illustrator, you could have been a typographer, you could have been a designer, you could have been a copywriter. I'm not sure you are any of them." Cheers Ken, but I think he was right in saying that I was a bit of an all-rounder, with no great strengths in any of them. When I later moved on to run a business I left all (or most of those skills) to the people who worked with me.

One other thing that Ken said, a standard 'exit' question I suspect: "What will be your ambition as a professional?"

"I'd love to design the graphics for the Olympic Games.", I replied, without hesitation. For some reason I was very clear even then on that ambition and, whilst I didn't quite achieve this and don't like 'second best,' I came as close as you can to this without really achieving it a - silver rather than a gold, maybe. More on this later.

During my final year at Bolton I came into contact with the Head of Design at Kellogg's. He was building his team and I was offered a job half way through my final year. This was a great luxury and I hope it didn't divert me from my college work. I did OK in the finals, but got a pass grade and no more, so who knows?

And so, after a couple of weeks off I went straight into gainful employment in the Summer of 1974. Kellogg's was a great start and perfect for me. Yes, I was employed as a designer, but more importantly I was pitched into the middle of working for a global brand. I think that it was my second week that I was sent down to London for a meeting at J. Walter Thompson's. I was scared stiff, but managed to pull it off with some help from an understanding art-director down there. But then he would be understanding, because I was 'the client.' Young, green, clueless, but still the client. Lesson number 1.

I was at Kellogg's for two and a bit years and again met some good people, as well as seeing how marketing works at a very high level. My boss, Dave Wilkinson, was – however – a bit eccentric. I doubt whether Dave is still alive, because he was a good deal older than me, but he looked after me as I'll tell in a moment. I also worked closely with the Kellogg's print buyer, Ron Yates. Not in the least bit eccentric, but totally pragmatic. Ron looked after me too and between him and Dave gave me a great 'post-graduate' training in the real world of commercialism.

But after a couple of years I was getting itchy feet. Kellogg's was great, but was naturally Kellogg's and nothing else (never was a company slogan 'if it doesn't say Kellogg's on the box, it isn't Kellogg's in the box' more appropriate) I applied for and was offered a couple of jobs, but didn't really fancy them for one reason or another.

Maybe the money wasn't as good as the fifty quid a week I was on. Yes, kids, that was a fairly good living wage in those days. But I didn't have to make a decision, it was made for me. Kellogg's brought a new managing director and several board members from the Canadian operation to re-jig the UK business. Within a week I and the rest of the design department, apart from the bosses, were made redundant. In Canada everything was outsourced.

Now this would have been easier to take if I hadn't just started paying my first mortgage, a huge £7,000. Dave Wilkinson and Ron Yates were devastated. It didn't directly affect them, as their jobs were secure. But they were good guys and felt everything personally for those of us who had lost our jobs. Within 24 hours another supplier of Kellogg's (fulfilment services for those famous Kellogg's free gifts with 10 packet tops etc.) had offered me free use of a small room over their little factory in Trafford Park and Dave and Ron had promised to 'outsource' my job to me – as instructed by their bosses...

It was in the days of magic markers, spraymount, scalpels and tracing paper. When I moved into that very basic room in Trafford Park it was November and a winter of freezing was ahead of me, to be followed by a summer of sweltering. (No heating. No opening windows.)

On the first night, after dark, Dave reversed his car up to the back door of the design studio at Kellogg's and, with me as watchman, nicked all of my equipment. And so it was, late on a dark November night that my first office and my first business were established. In a dump of an office with nicked gear.

True to their word, Dave and Ron fed my job back to me. But the difference was this time that in the first week I turned over 100 quid, rather than the 50 I had been on in proper employment. Yes there were some costs and expenses to come out, but I doubled my wages overnight. I still have that first job sheet somewhere and I think that my 'professional' rate was three quid an hour. Happy days!

But at the end of the first week when it came to sending out the bills, Ron worded me. "Listen son. You've just been made redundant from here, so you can't send bills in under your own name. So what are you going to call yourself?" I probably looked blankly at him and Ron probably suggested Trafford Design, which was what the business was instantly called. Not very original and could equally have been Trafford Cleaning Company or Trafford Car Servicing or any of the other Trafford somethings that are still listed in the phone book…or should I say on Google.

Now it wasn't easy by any means and, although I was enjoying the challenge of starting my own little business, there were long hours to work, equipment and materials to buy and, of course, there soon came the first foray with a bank.

Barclays in Trafford Park was just around the corner and I popped in very nervously to see the manager after a few months. I needed a piece of equipment, which we called a 'pram' – because it looked like a pram, with a hood. What it did, with the aid of two wheels on the front, was let you blow up images so that you could trace round them. Bloody hell. That and sticking layouts down with spraymount was as high tech as it got. This delightful piece of equipment was £700 and I needed a loan to buy it. The bank manager was charming and helpful (they were in those days) and tipped up the loan with no problem and I soon had my first piece of capital equipment. Within a few short years the capital equipment purchases would be fifty grandish.

Maybe I should have just stuck with the pram....but in this case the baby business outgrew it.

A few months on and I was now beavering away – the first of the 'nighters' under my belt to get the work out. I quickly realised that my first goal in business was to get more business in from sources other than Kellogg's. I knew that while it was good to have such a prestigious client, I couldn't rely on it for virtually all my turnover.

I've no idea now how I went about that process and I don't think for one moment that there was a 'sales plan.' I was and still am a lousy salesman. Some people are born to it, some people train to do it. I just can't. But I had met a lot of people during my two-and-a-bit years at Kellogg's and I was fairly well 'connected' even then, so step by step the business was starting to grow.

I was sales, design, art-work, delivery, client entertainment manager, cleaner and brewer upper. I even did some illustration work, which I enjoyed, but as Ken Adshead had said...well, you know what he said.

And around that time Ken phoned me to say that another of his ex-students was looking for office space and so one John Millington moved in with me. He had been an exceptional illustrator at college, although looking back he never utilised his talent to any great degree. John was not in the least bit pragmatic and couldn't sort out his life, his work or anything else. He just liked to paint and draw.

But he was good company and I thought the world of him. I need to time shift a little to get John's story complete. After a few months we formed a partnership, because what John did complemented what I did in those days. But he couldn't summon the strength to send an invoice, so I did that bit for us both. We took out a small wage from what was Trafford Design but became Trafford Design and Illustration just a couple of years later. When his marriage folded up, John was 30 years old and useless on his own as I have said. I saw the start of what would kill him 20 years later when he started on the Scotch.

During the following 15 years or so John worked with and for me several times, disappearing for stretches, re-appearing for stretches, but always falling deeper and deeper into alcoholism.

After further business growth, we were in our own, owned building and it had to come to a head when he 'hid' a bottle of Scotch in the bin under his desk. He would periodically 'drop' something so that he had to crawl on the floor to get it, sadly a typical alcoholic's behaviour, convincing himself that nobody was noticing.

He had to leave and I rarely heard from him for the following five years. Then one day I got a phone call to say that he had died. He'd been found dead, alone in his flat with a ruptured liver and had been there for some days. I thought the world of John, although many people perceived that we had fallen out. His funeral was obviously very sad and the waste of an unfulfilled talent was tragic.

But we did have a lot of laughs together as the business grew steadily. New clients were coming on board and the time had come to find a better environment. This has always been and always will be a hobby-horse of mine. I like interiors, working and living environments. I genuinely believe that people work better in good environments.

Now that might seem obvious, but remember this was the late 1970s/early 80s, when the swish interiors and exteriors we are all used to today weren't even on the agenda.

 But they were on mine... I found a nice little office above a bank on the main Chester Road into Manchester. It was my first proper lease, leased directly from the bank, so John and I had to go in to see the manager with our accounts and to be interviewed as 'fit and proper.'

This was just my second encounter with a bank manager and this time he was post lunch pissed (another norm for that period of the last century). We saw him write our names down on a Post-it, knowing himself that he wouldn't otherwise remember them. And then we saw his confusion as he put his coffee mug down on it, Post-it sticking to the mug's bottom as he picked it up again, where it stayed for the rest of the interview - adding to his growing confusion. He granted the lease, but I'm sure he didn't know much about doing so or who we were.

We spent (relatively speaking) a good bit on decorating and furnishing the reception area. Actually the reception area was the biggest part of the office suite. As always with me, I was trying to create a good impression. Within a few months we had a couple of employees (one who stayed for 20 years) and a series of lowly paid and utterly useless receptionist/administrators.

I wasn't good at being selective for that kind of employee and we actually weren't big enough to warrant needing a receptionist. It looked good though, being shown into a nice reception area and made to feel at home by a pretty girl – while four of us were crammed into a back room half the size of that reception...

I really can't remember how, but we made contact with Piccadilly Radio's sports reporter, Tom Tyrrell. Now Piccadilly Radio was massive in the region – the first of the independent stations – and Tom was the reporter for Man United, so I was pretty excited at this breakthrough. To us Tom was a celebrity. (Years later I waved nonchalantly to Tom at United's training ground as I walked past him into the private players' restaurant where he wasn't allowed to go.) But we began to do work for Piccadilly and, looking back, that started a rise in the profile of the business.

Whoa. Hang on a minute. Piccadilly and others on the horizon weren't going to want to deal with 'Trafford Design and Illustration.' It all sounded so parochial. We'd have to go back to the drawing board to 're-brand' as it would be called today. Perfect. The name of the business changed to Drawing Board. And soon after, Drawing Board became Drawing Board Limited.

Two years on and our small team had grown to a slightly larger team and we would have to find new premises. To be honest this was a bad time. I struggled and struggled to find somewhere suitable that we could afford. In the end another design based business – run by two of my part time tutors from college – offered shared space with them in Cambridge Street, near to the city centre. I was never comfortable with the loft space that they – we – occupied during that period. Today that loft is swish apartments. In the early eighties it was the top floor of a mill. Mind you, just around the corner Tom Bloxham had converted a small working space called Sally's Yard into very swish apartments. His first development. "Looks nice Tom," I think I remember saying to him, "But it'll never work in Manchester."

Although I wasn't happy with the space, this was a good time for the business as we drew in more clients, better clients, more high profile clients. They seemed to like the quirkiness of us working in a loft – and the business grew. I met some good people while working for Piccadilly Radio and extended my network of contacts enormously, mainly through the station.

Brian Beech was one of them. He was head of marketing at Piccadilly, which as he will freely admit meant organising T-shirts and printed balloons in those days. The irascible Beechy is still one of my closest friends. We're not bosom buddies, but we've been through a lot of crap each in our own time and we've always been there or thereabouts when really needed. (Thanks Brian. Now we're both grumpy old men.)

I gave Trevor Johnson his first proper job. He would never admit this now that he is so – quite rightly – high profile after all the great design work he has subsequently created. But his portfolio at interview contained primarily designs for seaside underpants. One notably bearing the legend on the (Y) front saying: 'I've got a lovely bunch of coconuts.' Admit it Trev, it was a long time ago, before Factory Records was invented.

But then Factory was invented and somehow a bit of a tetchy relationship came about, with the founding partners (no names, no pack drill etc…and no Tony Wilson evident at that stage) often gate crashing our commercial environment and demanding to see Trevor, who was also working for them freelance, producing album sleeve designs.

If we'd known how successful they were going to become, I suspect we'd have made them feel very at home. I didn't meet Tony Wilson until a couple of years later; to me, he was just a cub reporter on Granada.

So, things were growing. Not like topsy, but pretty steadily. I was still handling all the admin and everything else to do with the day to day running of the business. I - we - needed help. Since the days 'over the bank' we had done work for a company called Gordon Clark Publicity. They had a print buyer called Robert Sutton. To be honest offering Bob a job was also a good way to get him off our back as a client.

Pedantic. What an understatement. Rigorous. Ahem. Obsessive with detail.

Absolutely. We did pretty good art-work, but never, ever got anything past Bob first time as a client. So I offered him a job, he accepted and we lost a long-standing client.

Now Bobby revolutionised us. He made us put work into job bags. He made us give purchase order numbers before we ordered anything. He made sure that our art-work was even better than we had done for him – and he terrorised our repro suppliers and printers. I still see some of the printers of that day and mention Drawing Board. None of them remember me much, but every single one of them takes a sharp intake of breath and says, "Bob Sutton." And then most of them tell about their trepidation at bringing their work into him to check. And nobody EVER got anything past him first time. Sound familiar? It was bloody great to have him on our side.

I don't think anybody I've ever met has had anything but respect for wee Bobby Sutton and it was a great joy to work with him for 20 years. I was never quite sure whether Bobby was winding us up and wasn't really as pedantic and careful as he portrayed. No. On reflection he wasn't portraying anything. He was just like that. He was also endearingly mean: every day of those 20 or so years he brought a butty box into work with a jam-butty, a yoghurt and an apple in it. EVERY day for 20 years.

Occasionally we would buy him a new butty-box for his birthday and he would use it until we bought him another one. Like the brief case with one clasp which he tortuously carried round with him for years until we bought him another one. But best was probably his jacket. From day one he took his suit jacket off as he arrived in work (to preserve it) and put an anorak on. EVERY day. Now this was OK at first, but after 15 years it got a bit minging. Bobby (pristine in every other way) didn't seem to mind this. But one Friday afternoon he went on holiday, hung his minging jacket up on the same coathanger it had lived on for ever and departed. On the Monday we resolved to buy him a new jacket and burn the old one. So we took it down from the hanger…and inside was pinned a note that said 'KEEP YOUR HANDS OFF THIS JACKET.'

Sixth sense? Just Bobby.

Years later I was looking at the wage list and said to Bob, "Do you realise that I'm only on 40 quid a week more than you?" "Yes," he replied, "but are you worth it?" Well that was me told.

But we were a partnership and Bob contributed to all aspects of the business. And his meanness? Well, he retired at 50 after stashing a wad for 20 years, so who got it right?

But on to developments. The business continued to grow. Staff came and went, but mostly stayed. The work we did improved – and varied. Notably the brand developed for Piccadilly Radio and the subsequent work on all aspects of their marketing.

This included their report and accounts, work on road-shows and liveries, even Beechy's T-shirts and balloons. Looking back it was another wacky time, with even joy rides in the Piccadilly 'Eye in the Sky' traffic report helicopter. This mainly consisted of a cursory glance at the traffic below and then heading, for example, north towards Bury so that we could time how quickly we could fly to Stockport town centre. All interesting challenges. Picc was, as mentioned, the first independent radio station in the country. The MD, Colin Walters, was largely responsible for the shape of independent radio today and has since retired to France.

I was bawled out of his office on more than one occasion; but then so were a lot of other people. But then the shenanigans throughout the station were legendary and probably libelous to transcribe even now.

During that time the girl reading the traffic news came to attention. Rebecca Want – Sexy Bexy – was given her own show and went on to present TV programmes on Granada and become a local celebrity. I mention all this because eventually she and Brian Beech settled down together and now have a young son called Isaac. Rebecca is also my eldest daughter's godmother. A small fact, but important. Rebecca is still working in radio to this day. Brian is still working in PR to this day. Allegedly.

Another account – bizzarely – was The Elvis Presley Fan Club. I haven't got a clue how we picked that one up, but had great fun working with the guy who ran it. Bizzarely, he went by the name of Todd Slaughter. It was a bit odd working with the nascent Factory Records and the ageing Elvis Presley Fan Club at the same time.

We did have some straightforward, commercial clients. But it was the daft ones that kept us sane. I remember that at one point we had one of the late Elvis' platinum discs on a shelf in the office, next to a framed piece (allegedly) of his shroud. Bob and I also had to attend an Elvis tribute concert at Wembley arena and it was disconcerting to sit ordinarily besuited amongst 10,000 people wearing white rhinestone jackets.

I've just Googled Todd Slaughter and he's still running the fan club. Wow. Maybe I'll take in a date for a tribute.

I'm guessing this period was up to about 1982. I got itchy feet again, Bobby and I took ourselves off into the wastelands of Manchester, mooching around the many derelict and abandoned buildings that were around at that time. We'd worked out that we could buy somewhere for what it was costing us in rent. So that was the mission. Eventually – and it was a tortuous search – we found a building in Canal Street, right at the heart of the city but in what had become a no-go area. It was empty, nobody wanted it, it was for sale, it was in a state. So off I went to a bank manager again.

It was pretty much the same routine as my first foray all those years before. Pleasant and helpful people – bank managers were then. It helped that we did have a track record of paying for capital expenditure on the basis that it saved us money to invest, so we invested. The 50 grand I mentioned earlier (if you've not forgotten) was to pay for in-house typesetting. We were spending about 20 grand a year on buying out typesetting and so it didn't take much working out that if we borrowed 50 it would pay for itself in two and a half years or so, AND improve our service and profitability. The funny thing is we kept that Linotronic machine for years after it became redundant. I just couldn't bear to put something that had cost that much into a skip. Nowadays I think that my iPhone is more powerful than that pallet sized piece of kit.

So, along with our colleagues, we bought the building at 44 Canal Street. It was the first occupied building on Canal Street at that time and we did a good, honest job of converting it into design studios. I felt much more at home now and had myself a nice big office to ruminate in and from.

Two significant journalistic events took place almost immediately. Well, one was significant. The Daily Mirror ran a double page centre spread entitled 'The Vice Centre of Manchester.' It was a picture of a working girl sitting on our doorstep. Not a great start, as we had (tongue in cheek) named the building 'The Design Centre.' The second and much more minor journalistic event was a piece in Cheshire Life (I think) about the refurbishment we had done to a derelict building. I still have that clipping and I said in the interview, "One day Canal Street will be full of café bars and restaurants. The city needs a vibrant canal side waterfront." I made that statement up at the time, of course. I'm not a prophet, but to my amazement within 10 years it came true and Canal Street became the focal point for the Gay Village. This last fact was due entirely to the Rembrandt pub being on the corner. I didn't predict that part.

Well we moved in and exactly at that time I persuaded Tony Forster to become our Creative Director. And exactly at that time Trevor Johnson moved on to start creating his own name in the business. I had dearly wanted Tony and Trevor to work together, but it was not be. I admire Trevor for what he has achieved since and, after many years, have seen him several times recently.

But having 'Fozzie' on board was great. He continued to teach and inspire us all – as he had done since college days and continued to do so during his 10-year tenure with us professionally. Sadly his illnesses continued, until in 1997 he had to retire though ill health. But more of Fozzie later.

Working life changed considerably from that point. I had insisted on having a gallery space in the refurbishment of 44 Canal Street. I don't really know why, but we had a relatively big building and I thought it would be good to be able to host exhibitions. Well, this came to an unlikely fruition very early on in our stay at Canal Street.

I had wandered over to the States on one of my other regular missions, which was being a groupie to famous designers. I haven't got a clue again how this started, but I had wandered into – for example – Pushpin in New York (with a bit of an intro from Fozzie), Saul Bass's studio in Los Angeles and several others (including Alan Fletcher and Pentagram) and just said, "Hello. I'm really interested in your work." I had avidly attended seminars on design since leaving college and maybe that was where this groupie tendency had come from. But it had its rewards...

Dinner at Dick's

In Connecticut recently (what a great opening line), we called to see our old friend Dick Hess, world famous illustrator extraordinaire. Having met up with Dick in England on several occasions, this was the first time we had taken him up on his invitation to visit him in his quaint New England home town of Norfolk.

And having just driven up from the aggression and hurly burly of Manhattan, it was instantly refreshing to call in at the Norfolk post-office to ask directions and experience the local post-master offering to emerge from behind his counter and drive up to the Hess homestead, whilst we followed in the hired Chevy.

The Norfolk post-master waved a friendly hand towards an inconspicuous gap in the trees, before turning around and leaving us with a final, friendly farewell. The gap in the trees was earmarked only with an equally inconspicuous sign reading '1310,' a strangely high number considering the low number of houses we had seen during our drive through Norfolk, but then this was the USA and the road did run through three states and a forest which afforded a view of only a strip of sky and trees, trees, trees for more than 1000 miles.

Plunging through the gap there was a feeling akin to pushing open the door at the back of C. S. Lewis's wardrobe as the track, two or three hundred yards long, wandered through the forest to launch Chevy, occupants and all onto a spectacular New England mountain side with a sea of rolling tree tops stretching tens of miles across a view generated, it seemed, by that brand of computer graphics which allows no flaws in nature or light.

We passed an Amish style barn, slowing down to look for signs of activity, but there were none. Ahead, through the trees, there was a glimpse of another building of strange constitution for this part of the world. Stone. Trying to make the Chevy tip-toe up to the building (a difficult concept, particularly on gravel) we crunched to a halt convinced that we were trespassing or at the very least had come across a private mountainside hotel.

There was a guy working on the porch roof. Now when I say porch, you have to understand that I mean the sort of porch that straddles the road so that you can drive the charabanc in and disembark forty-five passengers in the rain without anyone getting wet. "Excuse me," I apologised deferentially to the guy on the roof. This was, as an opening gambit, a really dumb thing to say because far from having to attract his attention, he had stopped work to watch us when we were still a hundred yards away. "Excuse me, does Dick Hess live here?"

He suggested that we talk to the housekeeper and so, ringing a doorbell which clanged in the distance somewhere, we eventually made contact with Marielle. Dick was not in, we were told, and was he expecting us? Just calling on the off chance we said, following the next question about where we had travelled from with the throwaway line "Manchester... England." Dick should have been back two hours ago and she had no idea where he was. I was instantly reminded he had once told me that he was known as the late Dick Hess.

Retreating gracefully, we left a note to say that we'd call back and turned towards the Chevy. The biggest bloody dog I had seen in my life was between us and the car. (Now I know where Stephen King got the idea for Cujo.) Marielle cheered us up. "Don't touch him," she warned, he'll bite you. In the face."

Dateline: Saturday, September 15th. Time: Tennish.

After an entertaining night at the Blackberry River Inn, being treated as VIPs in a part of the world where real English people are a rare species, we returned to Hess Towers to be greeted by the dog and Dick in that order.

The greeting was correspondingly at opposite ends of the welcoming scale. Dick was delighted to see us, but thought it eccentric that we should just call on the off chance from the other side of the Atlantic.

We explained that we were just passing. A moment of confusion ensued, unsure which side of the sweeping split staircase into the lobby we should follow (Ginger down one side, Fred down the other – you've seen the movie). As an instant comparison, I gauged that my house would have fitted into the lobby area three times, with room to spare.

The lobby, if that is the right word, was like a museum of American folk art (apart from the Cezanne), littered with full size carousel horses, carved wooden figures, Shaker furniture and the odd Stars and Stripes draped over the odd Amish bench here and there. Dick and his friend Susan (I'm sure it was Angie Dickinson, but she insisted on being called Susan) were having breakfast and poured the statutory huge quantities of coffee for us whilst we sat in the kitchen, furnished with a 40- drawer French folk cabinet bought in Quebec and a cooking range large enough to fry a thousand eggs in three minutes.

Within a similar period of three minutes we were invited to check out of the hotel and take residence in the English Wing – "You'll like it, there's a cathedral window," gatecrash the evening's dinner party and join Dick and Susan at the Society 'do' of the year in Norfolk, Connecticut after dinner.

Naturally we refused on all counts, protesting our intention to call in for coffee only; being unannounced and English we didn't do that sort of thing. Negotiations ceased with our agreeing to join them for dinner and for the Cole Porter evening, but returning to the hotel in the interim.

Dick was apparently delighted, relishing being able to tell his other guests that his English friends has just 'called in.' "They'll think," he explained, "like all Americans think, that you're either a Shakespearian actor or an Oxford Don." I resolved to keep the Mancunian accent under tight control for the evening.

Thankfully we had taken evening clothes on the basis of 'you never know.' For once I was glad that we weren't the sort of people who could travel around the world with just a duffle bag.

At six that evening we arrived for dinner, crunching to a halt alongside two other guests who introduced themselves as friends of Angie's (sorry Susan's) – Samantha Jo Zimmerman and Rhoda L. Zuckerman. Later conversations elicited that Samantha Jo was a young(ish) widow of an elderly and very rich Hungarian Prince husband. She did some voluntary work when staying at her apartment in Manhattan as opposed to her house in Norfolk, where everything was so organised there was no voluntary work to do

.

Rhoda L. was a medical school graduate attorney something or other. Samantha Jo elicited our contribution later on in the evening that to survive in Connecticut one had to have Jo, Bob or Ray behind one's name. (Try it, it sounds New England.) And Dick contributed with a story about himself, Lou Dorfsman, Seymour Chwast and Herb Lubalin speaking at a seminar in the deep South somewhere years ago, following which they had each been given a belt inscribed on the back in studs with 'Dicky Bob,' 'Lou Bob' and 'Herby Bob.' I find Seymour Bob a little difficult to live with.

Rhoda L. was called exactly that. She had no middle name, but her father has decided at her birth that she was to be an attorney and therefore would need an initial for her name on the door-plate. Rhoda L. Zuckerman.

Both of these ladies were quite wacky and great fun. We sat overlooking the valley at the opposite end of the lobby from which we had originally entered, sipping the obligatory Martinis and nibbling at half a stone of pate (which the dog later ate completely while our backs were turned) and other guests began to arrive. We were told that a ballet dancer was joining the party, so it was only half a surprise when Bruce arrived dramatically and, with a flourish of both arms, still holding the Martini he had been drinking in the car, shouted in a manner which I am sure you can picture, "Daaarlings!" Skipping down Ginger's side of the staircase he joined the party with much kissing, hugging and exclamation in as dramatically choreographed a style as would befit a professional ballet dancer.

But he wasn't the dancer. Oliver (the dancer) arrived two or three minutes later accompanied by his own, and Bruce's wife.

The party of 11 was accompanied by an interior designer specialising in importing Italian furniture – or was he the playwright? Dick made a dramatic late entrance to his own dinner party in his own house, emerging black-tied from the shadows of one wing or another. Conversation was eclectic and, for example, I listened for ages to talk of the relative characters of Bobby and Teddy when this lot were all kids together, before realising that I should add Kennedy to the forenames.

I held my own brilliantly, dropping in comments such as, "All the world's a stage," and "Alas poor Yorick, I knew him reasonably well."

Dinner was followed by a short drive to the 'Shed.' A beautiful timber music hall, built on the Norfolk common at the end of the last century. Alongside the Shed, in a giant open-sided marquee, we drank champagne for a while amidst the glitterati of Norfolk society, while Dick and I swapped notes about our backgrounds. I am sure he enjoys his lifestyle and the friends that go with it, but treats the whole scenario with at least an air of arm's length. As a kid, he told me, unlike probably most of the other people there that night, his folks were well off because his dad was a milk-man and that was a regular job. Much more than his contemporaries had had during the depression.

Drifting to our seats in the Shed, we each found a bag of truffles left there for us to munch delicately through the performance. Rhoda L. and Samantha Jo canvassed the guests for spare goodies to consume and, all of us just having eaten dinner, polished off pounds of truffles that nobody else could face. The concert consisted of the entire collection of Cole Porter songs, sung by a chap we were told is 'World famous all over America' for doing just that, plus the Norfolk Music Society Ensemble. The culmination of the evening came with him singing the Yale College Song (written by Porter) accompanied by at least two thirds of the male portion of the audience who, it turned out, had been 'Yalies' and good American college boys to boot.

This dinner-suited accompanying audience swayed enthusiastically to their own rousing chords, a living vestige of the all American dream, remembering college days at Yale where the Stars and Stripes were mighty and, if there was even a hint of Vietnam and conscription, one sang the anthem from the Canadian side of the border...as Dick informed me.

Back in the car it seemed a jolly good idea to call at Angie's (sorry, Susan's) house and collect a chocolate cake before going back to Dick's and opening a couple of bottles of champagne. When we arrived back it seemed that there was something to celebrate because Samantha Jo had sold her house to Bruce and Tracy, his wife, during the time we had stopped off for the chocolate cake. Susan offered her services as attorney and everyone was happy.

Guests drifted off, Dick disappeared with a torch to put his pet cow away and returned mud spattered with a ruined pair of patent leather shoes on. We thanked our hosts and left, with them insisting we return for brunch in about five hours. Being English we declined politely. After all, we had only called in for a coffee.

"You're welcome to stay with us any time you are in England," we insisted. "Look forward to seeing you," replied the happy hosts.

Does anyone know if it's possible to hire Chatsworth for a long weekend?

Post Script: Sadly Dick fell ill a year after our visit and died in 1996. A true gentleman, he never did get to visit us at Chatsworth.

So we had a secretary at the time called Pam Shaw. And enthusing on my return from being a groupie in the States one day, Pam said, "Why don't we invite them over here to do a seminar for us?" Now a lot of people to this day think that the design seminars were my idea. Maybe I would have got there eventually with that, but it wasn't me who suggested it, it was Pam. So we invited world famous designers to come to Manchester to speak to us, our clients and our friends in the business. And they said yes.

It was the start of four or five years of design seminars that took place over three evenings each summer and featured some remarkable names from the world of design: Seymour Chwast, Paula Scher, Tony DiSpigna, Ricardo Rousselot, Dick Hess and so many more. It was at this time that I also first properly met Tony Wilson. Factory was burgeoning (creatively if not financially) and Tony was now a serious features presenter on Granada. Design was, of course, right up his street and he featured the design seminars on Granada each year.

I was like a pig in the proverbial and amazed that all these world famous designers agreed to come. And they were lovely to be with. All we paid were their air-fares and a cheapish hotel for three or four nights. And, naturally, we showed them the Manchester life of the time, which was starting to grow in fame under Tony Wilson's unplanned, unknowing creation of Madchester. We all sat in the Beaujolais restaurant one lunch-time and on the paper tablecloth (not so de rigueur) Tony DiSpigna and Ricardo Rousselot began to doodle, draw lettering.

Fozzie was, of course, part of our party and after a while they both said, "Come on Tony. Do your stuff. You inspired us in the first place." Reluctantly the ever self-effacing Fozzie did so. I still have that paper tablecloth to this day.

The nicest of the lot was Dick Hess. He chatted about how his dad had been a milkman in the great depression and was the only one in his entire family to have a job. He berated us for booking him a hotel – he would have happily slept on the studio floor. He coolly took a phone call from his secretary back in New York who was panicking because a client was on the way to see him there. "Just tell him I've popped out," he told her. He gave the game away just a little when he said, "I live in Connecticut and drive to New York on a Monday morning. Then I try to earn enough during the week to get my Porsche out of the parking lot on a Friday afternoon." Only a few short years later Dick died suddenly. But in the meantime I had had the privilege (and the awe) to visit him at his home in Connecticut and I hope that you have read my diary of that visit.

Perhaps because of this profile we kept picking up clients. Most notable were Reebok, for whom we worked intensively for 10 years or more. Apart from the work we did, this led to a Boy's Own dream of working not only with my beloved Manchester United (and waving to Tom Tyrrell nonchalantly as I went into the players' restaurant) but many other clubs and world famous footballers and athletes. I'll tell some of that story later.

But in 1988 Manchester made a bid for the Olympics. I noticed it in passing because there was not much more to notice in passing - just nominal coverage in the Manchester Evening News and a bit on the telly. It had been planned by Bob Scott, later to become a mentor of mine, although he doesn't know that to this day and I doubt whether he will be reading this. But naturally my ears pricked up.

We looked into it a little and found that the design work for the bid had been done by a London company. None of us on the Manchester scene were best pleased. Now another groupie hero of mine was East End turned Hollywood designer, Arnold Schwartzmann. Not Schwarzenegger – he was too bald, too fat and too Jewish to be mistaken for The Terminator. Arnold had done most of the design work for Rolling Stones albums in the 70's and 80's (A time when I also groupied in on Michael Peters and Partners, admiring them in the UK more than any other design group – but again more later.)

But Arnold was probably most famous for being the Creative Director for the Los Angeles Olympics in 1984. So let's invite him to do a seminar in our gallery in Manchester. And let's invite Bob Scott along and let's have a go at Bob about why our City was being represented globally in an Olympic Bid using London designers. Bob, to give him his credit, turned up. So did Tony Wilson with his Granada camera crew and pointedly asked Bob in the interview why he hadn't used Manchester designers. "Because," he said, "I didn't know they were here." Ah. Fair point. Now many of our colleagues were at this gathering and heard this. They were erstwhile rivals from design businesses such as The Chase and Creative Lynx and others, but all were friends in the cause because this was how Manchester worked. So we, and they, got together to form (after prolonged debate) The Manchester Design Community. To try and make sure that people did know we were here and fight back against the supposition that the only good design came from London. MDC was launched.

In that context the MDC lasted several years and ultimately – I understand – has evolved into and with the Manchester and Liverpool Design Initiative. I know very little about that organisation these days, but the MDC served as a good vehicle for several years. Notably when never, never give up Bob Scott decided to try again, for the year 2000 Olympics. He wouldn't have dared to go to London (Wilson would have had his guts for garters).

He came to the MDC. Now instantly another conundrum sprang up. The MDC were all 'rival' companies. So how do we handle a pitch for this prize? It was all dead good and altruistic in those days. Nobody wanted the British

Olympic Bid more than me. I'm sure everybody else wanted it too. So we had a beer or two and decided on an MDC strategy. We would all do our own design pitch, but allocate the work to another of our members to present. Voila.

Fozzie had worked his magic and produced a lovely design for the bid. It was presented to the Manchester Olympic Organising Committee by another member of the MDC (to be honest can't remember who and if I could, would love to give a name check) and....we won. Another wow. It was 1989 and Ken Adshead's 'exit' question in 1974 and my answer were uppermost in my mind. "What is your professional ambition?" "I'd love to design the graphics for the Olympic Games." Well not the Games, but a bid. And what was more, for my city. Fozzie had designed it, the team had delivered it. I had to manage it. But that was perfect. And then began a four year process of learning how these things work and delivering a bid for the year 2000 which was met almost universally with, 'Manchester? You're having a laugh!'

I worked in those very early stages with such a small team on the bid that inevitably grew through the subsequent four years. But there were a handful of people then. Half a dozen it seemed. Bob Scott at the helm, with Mike Dyble in charge of the marketing. We set to designing and delivering all of the marketing collaterals we were asked to and the most unnerving thing about those subsequent four years as I worked on the Bid almost exclusively, was a Post-it on the notice board of the Olympic Bid boardroom on Oxford Street - the only thing on the board - that just had my home telephone number on it.

I'll skip the Bid years a little. I travelled to Barcelona with the City for the 1992 Olympics. I travelled to Atlanta when they won the 1996 Olympic Bid. What an overall experience. But in the middle I'll tell a few stories about what I did when I wasn't 'Bidding.'

We were never that big as a business. Not as big as many perceived we were. At most we had around a dozen staff, maybe 15. People joined, some left. The industry was changing with the introduction of computers. I can't give everyone a name check and some either I wouldn't want to or they wouldn't want me to. I've made friends and enemies in life like everyone (except Fozzie, who only made friends), but most of the people I've worked with through the years I am still on good terms with or would be if I still saw them. It was all about the people that worked at Drawing Board. And it was good, but tough going like any business is.

The world only sees the exterior of business, not what happens day-to-day inside. But we were ploughing on. Around this time, with so much going on, an old college friend of mine joined the business as Production Manager. Tony Lomas stayed for many years, as many had done and did a sterling job in getting the work out. Of which there was more and more. Richard Pemberton joined as Sales Director, because we needed a Sales Director to keep pace with the spiral of growing.

I know that this sounds daft and probably was, but Bob and I were looking to turn over a million quid a year, but between us we couldn't quite hit it. But we got Reebok and Richard was a natural salesman, so he developed it to the level that it became. Perversely Reebok ultimately dominated the business in terms of turnover, just as Kellogg's had in the early days. Until we said, 'Oh-oh. Too many eggs in one basket again.' But it was a great account to have for 10 years or more. And it let me in to Man United...

There were many stories. I'll tell just one. Pretentious? Moi? Well, I went on a jolly some time in the 90's to the European Cup Final in Rome with Glenn from Reebok, Ryan Giggs – whom I'd worked with since he was 17 – and Andy Cole. Guess it must have been about 1994. Ryan's mate Dave was with us too. Sadly I'd got a bit blasé about my team by then and I remember being at a night match with Glenn. Afterwards he asked me if I fancied a drink in the players' lounge. "Nah," I said. "Too knackered." My Dad, I'm sure, turned in his grave at that moment.

Well on this jolly I had my own Champion's League car to run me around. They must have thought I was someone important, because I was with Ryan and Andy. Manc, working class with my own Champion's League car. (Come to think of it this had happened in a more minor way a little time before, but I'll do that story next, un-chronoligically and self contained.) So it was an interesting experience. But the highlight was a cameo when me, Ryan, Andy and Dave were wandering round the Coliseum. As you do.

Now Dave had been boring us all for a couple of days looking everywhere for a long sleeved Juventus shirt. They didn't really exist with long sleeves in Italy but Juve were playing Ajax in the final, so he wanted one. Suddenly he spotted a young guy wandering towards us – wearing a long sleeved Juve shirt. He nudged Ryan and nodded in the direction of the young guy. But as he drew near the young guy spotted our party and exclaimed (no other word for it), "Rrrryan Giggggs!" Dave immediately accosted him with, "Where-you-get-shirt?" to which came the reposte, "Manchesterrrrr!"

"No, you dozy bastard, we from Manchester. Where-you-get-shirt?" Young guy, "JJB Manchesterrrrr." Dave, perplexed at this scenario then asked, "Where-you-from?" "Llandudnoooo." Came the reply in a Welsh accent that had previously sounded so, so Italian. Well, laugh? I can still see Ryan sliding down the wall in the Coliseum with tears streaming from his eyes. Although this crying was to be repeated about an hour later after we had split up and then met up again outside the Coliseum. Paul Stretford (Mr. Smoothy and ex-Piccadilly Radio way back) was then Andy Cole's agent. (And is now Wayne Rooney's.) I found the same crew sliding down a wall at the foot of the main steps into the Coliseum again in tears. I had missed it but apparently Paul had tripped on the first of the two hundred steps down and only maintained his balance all the way down by careering through swathes of tourists who had had to leap out of his way.

Bless him. I've not seen Paul for years and years, but I do remember him asking me to bring back all of the shopping he'd done in Rome because he had forgotten that he wasn't going back to Manchester, but flying straight out to the States. The only time I've ever got on or off a plane carrying bags bearing the name of every mega profile Italian fashion designer. I usually do M & S.

And the unchronological story.... Reebok commissioned a TV ad when they signed Ryan up on sponsorship. It was the early days of computers remember and the theory was that the ad would feature United's greatest ever team, with footage of the chosen players 'matted' together to make them look like it was live action. Robert Fallow, the Glaswegian Reebok Marketing Director, (who had trained for this job driving a tank in the army. Honest!) asked me to pick the team. Now this was fantasy football extreme. So I did so, the only proviso being of course that Ryan was in it. It sort of wouldn't have worked as a Giggsy ad if he wasn't... I can't remember exactly what team I (and my sons) picked by poring over old programmes in our huge collection, although it featured Best, Charlton and... Giggs. The ad was voted best of the year.

Now there used to be a programme on the telly, hosted by Desmond Lynam, called 'How did they do that?' Shortly afterwards Robert Fallow called me in to say that Lynam wanted to do the ad and explain how it had all been put together with old footage and new computers. "I want you to be interviewed as an ordinary football fan who had won a competition to choose the team. Good PR for Reebok."

"Nope."

"We'll pay all your expenses."

"Nope."

"Do you want to keep this account?"

"Errr…"

So I was flown down to London to be filmed in close up sitting in the seats at Crystal Palace. Man United wouldn't let them film it at Old Trafford – conflict of sponsorship! The point of the story is that – on expenses – I came out of the terminal at Heathrow wearing a big coat and a big hat (it was the middle of winter) and hailed a cab. "Crystal Palace Football Club please." The cabby just said, "Nobody's said that to me since Malcolm Allison twenty years ago," and he was off on a mission, obviously wanting to regale his mates with how he had had a fare on the way to a British record signing. I kept schtum. One can't tell cabbies what one's business is or it might get into the press.

As we arrived at the ground he asked where I wanted dropping off and of course I said, "Directors' entrance please." He was thrilled and stayed to watch as I tried that door and it was locked. So I pretended to be checking my watch and checking the papers in my briefcase. But he stayed to watch. Eventually I gave up and went through the groundsman's entrance as I had been instructed. Well, I could just have been going into the ground incognito.

The main upshot of this episode was that for probably a year afterwards I couldn't walk into my local pub without some wag shouting, "How did they do that?"

There were many football stories and all gained working with players and clubs. Yes of course I miss that work and those times. But I'm far too old to do it now even if I was asked. I've told a couple here, I could tell a thousand more. But it was all a great experience. But one that I have to mention: I was working with the players at Anfield. We actually worked more with Liverpool than United over this period and one project was proving a bit stressful. Little Sammy Lee eventually said to me, "Come on Rich, let's go and have a cup of tea in the boot room." Now I worked all over Europe with some of the greatest of players. I had lunch once in the players' restaurant at Real Madrid...I worked with Dario Grady at Crewe...but the only time I got shivers down my spine was in the boot room at Anfield. The spirits of Shanks and Paisley are still there.

And I waved to Tom Tyrrell as I walked into the Man United players' private restaurant.

So all of this was happening before, during and after the MDC, the Olympic Bid pitch and four years of intensive work on that Bid. The Bid was for the Games in the year 2000 and are awarded seven years in advance, to enable the extraordinary level of planning and investment that goes into them. And what I very quickly learnt and what leads to so much controversy about Olympic Games funding is that they are a catalyst for regeneration, much more than a sporting event.

Much of the work I would do in subsequent years would be with this in mind and I have spoken both privately and publicly on this subject. When doing so I try to explain and understand – which I do – how there can be such opposition to these events.

Take Barcleona. A city, I learnt, with massive sociological and geographical problems that stretched back many decades through the manufacturing decline of the 20th century. The award of the Games of 1992 instantly led to a public and private sector injection of capital which transformed the city in a time scale that would have taken decades without that focus. Look at Barcleona today. Just over twenty five years ago it was a city of dereliction, social problems, economic stagnation and strife. Not that it doesn't still have its problems. Every city does. But the Games transformed Barcelona.

Now what other city comes to mind with dereliction, social problems, economic stagnation and strife late in the 20th. century. Well at least one was Manchester. And so it dawned on me what this could achieve, or help to achieve. And my passion as a Manc took over.

Now it wasn't all straightforward and as I'll tell, the ultimate outcome of the British Olympic Bid wasn't successful, but it catalysed the City – after most Mancs had stopped laughing at the prospect, which came several years later. The Bid started a belief that we could do things. Or rather amplified a belief that had started with Tony Wilson, Factory and Madchester. >Manc cheek. >Manc self deprecation. >But Manc. And yes, the IRA bomb of 1996 further hastened the process. But all of these things were parts of a cog that had started to go round.

As mentioned, in the early days – 1988/1989 – there were a tiny handful of people involved: Bob Scott (mentor: "If you ask me I'll stick my nose in. If you don't I'll just let you get on with it."), Mike Dyble, Fran Toms and Penny Boothman of the City; Jim Chapman of BDP and a few others. I vaguely remember sitting round tables drawing scribbles of where we could put a stadium. 'This bit's really run down. Bradford Gas Works was there. How about putting a stadium there? And an indoor arena. Well, there's a bit of ground that's not being used next to Victoria Station. Maybe it could go there?' And I have recollections of sitting in the stadium in Barcelona three or four years later with Penny, trying to count how many seats there really were, because we reckoned they had fibbed.

So we did our bit. A good brand and lots of 'marketing collaterals' as they (I) would say today. We broke ground with the new computers. We worked hard, we fell out, we made friends. We worked hard again. We got our City on our side and a little belief started, mainly due to Bob, whom I shadowed all over backing him up with the things he needed to show people to prove that we were serious.

He was extraordinary as an Olympic Bid orator. I remember one occasion when he turned up at the Manchester Business School to speak to a full house. He arrived one minute before he was due to start and as he strode passed me asked, "Who is the audience? What are they here for? What do they expect to hear?" I think I gave him the benefit of the content of the 'marketing collaterals' we had been working on for the event in the 30 seconds or so that I had and, as always, he went on to talk inspirationally with no notes, for an hour or more.

We had to submit our Bid to the IOC in 1993 – seven years before the year we were bidding for. But before that we had to produce what was known as the 'Technical Bid Document.' This had to be presented a year in advance of the IOC's synod to make a decision and so at the start of 1992 we began work on that, the major piece of presentation work that had to be done.

In the years immediately prior to 1992 there had been considerable corruption scandal within the IOC. This led them to brief that Technical Bid Documents should be produced in the most economical way possible, recyclable (early Green) and basically with no frills. (Perhaps this had something to do with one bidder for a previous Games delivering its bid in and as part of a fully stocked cocktail cabinet!) Now the world had started to think and talk desktop publishing. Yes, so short a time ago and nascent computers were leading people to believe that they could design on them with no training.

So we set out to do something which we didn't really understand, using some equipment which was basic and we sort of understood a bit, on a project which nobody had a clue how to do. Not a great starting recipe, but we had no choice in the matter. (As it ultimately turned out, none of the other bidding cities paid a blind bit of notice to any of these IOC 'rules.')

After the initial planning, which largely consisted of 'what the hell do we do?' we started work on the document. We had nine months to produce the thing and we didn't have a clue how long it would take. We soon learnt that it would take nine months. When we sort of analysed it we reckoned it would be about 500 pages long and would effectively constitute the first master plan for the City of Manchester.

What we did work out early on was that we had to obtain copy and content from something like 52 local and national governmental organisations. These included, for example, information from climate conditions through to what time the buses stopped running at night. All of that gathered, designed and put together, checked and signed off by each department, it then had to be produced 'economically' in English AND French. Bugger. Nowt to do but just get on with it. So we talked to Rank Xerox, who had chucked their weight behind things as a sponsor, we talked to Jim Chapman and BDP, who were the master planners and we talked to the Town Hall, who gave us somewhere to work. Somehow I was in the middle of this and the only one who knew – or was supposed to know – what was going on with each bit and joining all the bits up from a team of 25.

What we did with the help of all these people was 'Create and revolutionise the new world of desk-top publishing,' and that was according to a major feature on the Bid in the Guardian. So it must have been true. What effectively it meant was that we were taking shedloads of information and turning it into something that was clear, legible, well designed and then finding a way to print it out on Rank Xerox equipment. Sounds so easy today, but it couldn't readily be done in those days. And print a piece of paper both sides. Hmmm. 'We're not sure. We'll test it and see if it works.' A couple of years previously a rookie from college had joined Drawing Board. A lad by the name of Adam Varnom. He seemed promising and had taken on the mantle of learning how to use the first computers we had bought. So Adam and I set to the task of creating a design and producing the first few pages.

We were obviously a lot younger then and too green to do a runner from the whole prospect. As it turned out we lived at the Town Hall for nine months. Well at least I went home for five or six hours (including travel) every day for those nine months. Adam had a suite at the Midland (another sponsor who'd come on board) because that meant he didn't have to lose an hour travelling home and back. I think that we had Christmas Day and half of Boxing Day off, but other than that we worked around 18 hours a day, every day of the week for nine months.

Lots of people, from Rank Xerox to BDP, put in the mind numbing hours. But Adam put in more than me only because he didn't have travelling time to account for. And just to add for good measure, someone belatedly informed me that we hadn't actually made a Bid yet, just an intention to Bid. When the Bid document was actually delivered to the IOC Headquarters in Lausanne and signed for, then that was when Manchester had made a Bid. If it wasn't delivered and signed for by 1pm on the designated day, then the Bid was declared null and void. Which was how I felt when I heard this fact. Why I hadn't picked it up in the previous three or four years I'll never know. I'd hazard a guess that none of the team knew this though, right from Bob down. We were all rookies. The Government had, by this time, put five million quid into the Bid and I had instant visions of missing the deadline, thereby dumping Manchester's Bid to oblivion and having my tax code altered to 'Emergency' until the day I died (or was lynched).

It got more and more complicated to produce as we delved deeper and again I was in the position of being the only person who knew how all the bits fitted together. Rank Xerox management produced this high flying 'Critical Time Path Analysis' half way through, maybe to prove that it couldn't be done on time and certainly to convince me that only one person knowing all the bits was not good, to say the least. But I was too bloody busy to spare the time to read it. Sorry Rank Xerox, you were right, but I was too busy and certainly too stressed. By the end of the process I was literally hallucinating at times. A very disturbing experience and one that should have told me that Rank Xerox management were absolutely right. But I was too busy.

And talking of Rank Xerox, we had managed to speed their printers up to print a whole, full colour page in around a minute and a half. So, how many pages was this to be. Hmmm. Around 500. And how many copies did we have to produce for the IOC. Around 450. So 500 x 450, that's, errrm, 225,000 pages and it takes a minute and a half to print one page. Errrm. That's something like 5,625 hours just to print out. That's, let me see, about 234 days running 24 hours a day. Hmmmm.

No bloody wonder I was hallucinating.

And during this process I came across a young executive at the Town Hall. His name was Howard Bernstein and he seemed to be able to fix things, make them happen. Like when all the power died in the computer suite. "Had you all backed up?" I croaked. I then croaked down the phone to the maintenance department. I was told that they'd fill in a job sheet and get there as soon as possible. Probably tomorrow. I phoned Howard and croaked the problem to him. Two minutes later we heard the unmistakable sound of an electrician's feet running down the corridor. But my most endearing memory is of Howard wandering in towards the end of the process and picking up one of the pages from the Bid Document, which were all boxed ready for collating. He turned it over in his hand and then said to me, "I've been thinking. Maybe we should reprint this section on a different colour." I know that my eyes were utterly, completely expressionless as I looked back into his and said nothing for 10 seconds. "Forget it," he said.

We got there. Bob Sutton and I were somewhere off Oldham Road at three in the morning at the binders. Adam was probably back in the Midland having a drink and an all night pizza from room service. But we got there. It was Saturday night/Sunday morning and a private jet had been booked to take off with the first Tehnical Bid Documents and fly them to Lausanne. The jet was booked for 11 am and we packed the documents up for transit at 5 am. A year and we made the deadline by six hours.

The whole team met in the Midland that afternoon. I was out of it and lasted an hour. The rest of the team caroused until the evening and drifted off one by one. I did hear later that nobody had paid the bill. I think it stung the manager a bit, but they were sponsors.

The post script to all of this is that I got stick the following week from virtually everybody I knew, because the news broadcasts on the Monday night were edited to show me and Bob drinking champagne in the Midland and then me (wonders of editing) landing in a private jet in Switzerland. I wasn't there. I was comatose in bed at home.

There then followed a (relative) lull.

The Bid team, maybe 50 or 60 people by now, began to work their way through the Technical Bid Document and through the many visits of the IOC representatives who came to Manchester over subsequent months to check that what we had put in the document were either correct, or deliverable if we got the Games. We all knew that Manchester wasn't there yet, but we had the example and the inspiration of what had happened to Barcleona to push us on. They had seemed unlikely candidates, but then their ace was that Juan Antonio Samaranch was both the President of the IOC and from Barcelona. I actually had a fleeting conversation with Samaranch....about Manchester rain. I think that we were at a school in Didsbury during his one visit. Mandatory visit I guess, being a candidate.

And on the subject of rain: while we were in Barcleona I hunted down Javier Mariscal and managed – as a groupie – to get to see him in his studio. The brand for the Barcleona Games had been developed by Josep Trias. Now it was a good, workable design, suited to the Barcelona image and sunshine. It was based on adaptable abstract patterns representing the tile work of Antoni Gaudi on the Sagrada Familia and various other features in Barcelona.

But the city had been captivated by Cobi, the mascot for the Games, created by Mariscal years before and subsequently adopted by Barcelona as their 'representative.' Cobi was a dog. A simplistic, cubist, anarchic comic book character that was as easy to draw as Mr. Men and had a character that was built over years. All Barcans were familiar with Cobi long before the Games, perhaps as an underground sort of symbol of rebellion.

I like smoothies and am always impressed by them. Shallow I know, but the kind of 'smoothness' is always different. Mariscal was perhaps the smoothest of all. I was welcomed into his studio and shown up a flight of stairs in an old factory. The factory was crumbling beautifully as only factories can in Mediterranean climes. Crumbling plaster looks beautiful dappled by sunlight. In Manchester it just looks 'orrible.

All the work and his team were on the ground floor and when I topped the stairs and reached his 'office' I saw one desk in the centre of maybe 10,000 square feet of space. Right in the middle. And above it, upside down as a huge light fitting, was a fairground carousel complete with lights. Smooth. Mariscal said 'Hello' and asked if I would like a coffee. I said yes and he buzzed downstairs. Two minutes later a goods hoist platform next to his desk descended from view and returned a few seconds later with one cup of coffee in the middle of it, right slap bang in the centre. Now that's smooth.

We chatted and he explained how Cobi worked in the context of the Barcleona Games. The character was 'alive' and as such there was no 'official' version. Every Barcelona business could have their own Cobi and were encouraged to do so to show their participation. For a fund raising fee they commissioned Mariscal's studio (it had to be done officially) to draw them a Cobi. The ground floor of the factory was full of staff drawing Cobi's to order. Two minutes with a couple of magic markers and a sense of humour and it was done.

So Cobi was everywhere. Everywhere. The Josep Trias graphics were just a working backdrop to Cobi World. Cobi brought the City and the Games to life and everybody related to him and owned him. Or their own version of him. He could be anything you liked: funny, serious, daft, business like. All things to all Catalans, so to speak. There was no signing off process, it would never have worked that way. Everybody owned Cobi. I didn't see it, but heard afterwards, that the day after the Barcelona Games tens of thousands of citizens attended a closing celebration and were asked to go to the beach (which before the instigation of the Games had been inaccessible and derelict. Regeneration.). There were a few formal speeches and ceremonial things and then a 30-foot high inflatable Cobi emerged from the sea and was released to float upwards and out of view into the sky. There wasn't, I heard, a dry eye on the beach. Cobi was saying goodbye. What a piece of theatre.

Mariscal and I had a friendly chat for half an hour or so and as I left he drew me a Manchester Cobi. Complete with bowler hat, suit and an umbrella.

Perceptions. But that Manchester Cobi is the only one that exists.

Several months later, towards the end of 2003, we had to present to the full IOC in Monte Carlo. The decision would be made on that day. Of course activity stepped up again and virtually the whole team was mobilised with a job to do for our great opportunity. I am an inveterate diary keeper and, of course, kept a diary of those days in Monte Carlo. I think that it is the only complete – although personal and therefore entirely subjective – record of what happened in those days. I hope that you have the stamina to read it, having got this far, although you will already know that we didn't win the Bid.

Manchester takes on the Olympic World in Monte Carlo

Sometimes, when you least expect it or have not carefully considered it, or have maybe been too embroiled in a situation to realise what you are getting into, you have an experience which you know will never be recreated as long as you live. I have just had such an experience and a reluctance to relate it comes from nervousness that I will not be able to recreate the time, the place, or the atmosphere in words.

I feel desperately lucky to be involved, if in only a small way, with one of the most incredible scenarios in the world. After years of watching from the sidelines and not – as one cannot from the outside – understanding the processes involved, almost three years of competing in the longest marathon of all came to fruition when I was with the competing team at the finishing line.

At the moment my fear of being unable to recreate the finish in words is tempered by wanting to try and explain the experience to those who were not lucky enough to be there after running alongside me during those three years. I hope that I will write a full account of those years later. At the moment memory is fresh and should, perhaps, be written down before the detail is lost.

On the morning of September 21st 1993, I joined the party at Manchester International Airport, waiting to be flown to Monte Carlo for the decision by the IOC of who should host the Olympic Games in the year 2000. The flight having been laid on by British Airways as part of their sponsorship, checking in was quick and informal, with each and every one of the party being treated as a VIP, including quite rightly the group of Manchester school children and their teachers who would later take the Casino Square by storm with their own brand of song and steel drum music.

They were streetwise kids who bubbled with excitement that just occasionally showed through their ingrained matter-of-factness to life. I spent a few minutes taking in the noise and sensing the atmosphere of 'de-mob' happiness that pervaded the concourse, with one or two of the Bid staff involved in organising the kids and latecomers to the flight – of whom I was inevitably one. My further delay involved waiting for the last delivery from the office of supporting material ordered by telephone from Monte Carlo the previous day.

Once everything was in hand I made my way to the Bridgewater Suite to join the rest of the party waiting for the flight. After so much extensive work in different areas by so many people and groups, the assembly gave a glimpse of the carnival that was to be part of Monte Carlo for the next four days.

Coffee and biscuits, red, white and blue panama hats, scarves and bags, were handed out to the assembled team. Many familiar faces were outnumbered by more who were unfamiliar – and a passing conversation between Jim Chapman and me did express some doubt as to who had been as involved as ourselves and who was just along for the expensive ride. John Glester, Chief Executive of CMDC, called the assembled group to order and briefed us in how the Bid was being viewed in Monte Carlo and at home, with instructions on the part which we were all to play when we arrived. The main message was, inevitably, to do with the media of each country, who were desperately searching for a chance or off-the-cuff word from one of the bidding teams or their supporters.

Particular aggression in this area, we were told, was coming from the Australian press with their country having, it felt, peaked a little early in their campaign and now being left to look for the downside of their competitors to make the headlines.

The British Bid was looking good, with (master tactician) Bob Scott having us placed exactly where intended a year ago – snapping at the heels of Beijing and Sydney in the final straight with them having expended their best ideas and energy before the final push. The carnival flight left with an air of confidence – although the unified screams of 50 musical kids as the 'plane lifted off finally broke through their determination to promote the streetwise above the new experiences of youth.

Two very untaxing hours later and the contingent was on the tarmac at Nice, checking swiftly through immigration to the baggage reclaim hall. Within a minute of our arrival the power failed in the hall, dousing the lights and stopping the conveyor to dark mutterings of "it's an omen..." a phrase used throughout the following days as the group became more and more edgy while the deadline approached. Every minor occurrence was greeted with speculation about the gods being on our side, or steadfastly forming a front row to stop us in the culmination of the long quest.

The kids from Moss Side and Whalley Range soon dispelled the temporary gloom by breaking into a series of songs which were to become very familiar over the next 48 hours.

Onto the transfer bus and into the haven of air conditioning to ease the blast of Southern European heat which had assailed our first half hour out of the 'plane and a seat with a face who had run some of the way alongside the Drawing Board team: Janet Harrison had produced the final film sequences for the presentation. These sequences had so far been kept completely under wraps ready for the big moment.

And there were one or two other familiar faces – with, in the case of Rob Green from BT, the most spectacular pair of ears I had come across in our work on the Bid. Undaunted as ever, the pocket sized telecommunications expert demonstrated how his Bid panama hat appeared to have been supplied with a pair of joke appendages fixed skilfully below the rim.

The compact radar dishes, however, demonstrated their own true fixing when the hat was removed, by staying firmly fixed to the place where I had previously noted them with some wonder on our first meeting at the Olympic Salute over a year ago and on our subsequent meetings.

Another brief encounter came in a ridiculous conversation with Ian Topping who, it later transpired, had been instrumental in the placing of the famous five acre flower logo at the airport. He introduced himself by name and I reciprocated, adding the question 'SEMA?' onto my name. Completely and not illogically assuming that I was from SEMA and not that I was asking if he was from that information technology company, we began our time together each thinking that we were from the company that each of us assumedly worked for, but neither did.

Through the rolling hills of the South of France the coach entered the principality of Monaco and wound down the spectacular harbour side and through the town of Monte Carlo to the Congress Hall, where we all had to obtain our IOC accreditation. All of the necessary information having been supplied several weeks earlier back in the UK, the process was relatively smooth and we boarded our coach again, with members of other cities' delegations eyeing us somewhat suspiciously. The thin film of ice was soon to be broken as delegates from around the world relaxed very quickly in each other's company.

(I also later learned of the amusement of another British party, who had all checked in at a nearby hotel obviously earmarked for the uniformed branch. They had all travelled to Monte Carlo together, all dressed in civvies and none of them knowing what their travelling companions were there for. On reassembling that evening there was a complete collection of uniformed British bobbies, Scottish pipers, the Band of the Coldstream Guards and Dennis, the Town Cryer from Sandbach.)

A mile down the road and we checked in at the Beach Plaza Hotel. Up to the sixth floor in the lift, a short struggle with the digital key and the bags dropped on the floor before walking straight out on to the balcony overlooking the private beach and terrace, with a small assortment of swimming pools. There, at the end of a headland a couple of hundred yards away, was the Monte Carlo Sporting Club, where our fates would be decided in two days time.

We had all been invited to a reception and dinner at the Metropole Palace that evening, as guests of the Monte Carlo ex-pats society. This broadly translated as guests of what is probably the richest private club in the World; there are 1,200 British tax exiles in a total population of 30,000 who inhabit Monaco. Of that 30,000, we were later to learn, only 5,000 are French. These unfortunate souls are the only ones who pay tax in the principality.

The group of Brits who began to assemble in the bar an hour later were definitely not tax exiles, but numbered, to my disquiet, a section of North Western society instantly recognisable by bluff Northern attitudes and accents to match: Salt of the Earth Mancunians who had contributed to the Bid and were now along as supporters to see it through to the final stage. There seemed to be a proliferation of garden centre owners and their spouses, determined quite rightly to have a good time and to start straight away. I grouped with three IT men from SEMA and Janet, all of us now refreshed from our journey and ready to do our British bit in Monte Carlo.

After an hour in the bar, our group decided to do the proper thing and see if the transport to the Metropole had arrived. It had – and left again. One of the SEMA men went back into the bar to relay the news to the bunch of horticulturalists (is that the correct collective noun?) who were by now having such a good time that I was not sure whether they were going to make the reception at all.

We got a cab to the Metropole and through reception out on to the terrace, where a throng of people had already gathered. I was stunned by the scene of azure evening sky behind the darkened Monte Carlo skyline of Disneyesque buildings and palm trees. And, in the middle of the elevated terrace, a gently lapping swimming pool with a huge Bid flag floating in the middle, discreetly anchored in the spotlights. I marvelled to Janet at the graphic qualities of the scene and she confided to me that one of the shots in her film involved a swimmer diving into a pool, on the bottom of which was a Bid logo. I was intrigued.

The assembled collection of tax-exiles, politicians and world famous sports stars milled around the pool glittering, a little like a human version of one of those mirrored globes that adorned the old time dance halls. Jim Chapman, Janet and myself were talking by the pool, trying not to look conspicuous by lack of glamour, when we were seized upon by Mike Dyble, photographer in tow, who said he wanted a picture of his 'design team' together – architecture, films and graphics. Although a little taken aback by this we complied. As we stepped back a pace to make an attractive grouping for the camera, an image flashed through my mind of taking one step too far and very ungracefully falling backwards into the flag bedecked pool. I could hear through an imaginary water logged sensory system, someone saying, 'Who's thet in the pool, deah?' to the reply, 'Oh don't worry, deah, it's only the designah.'

Dennis, the Town Cryer from Sandbach, suddenly appeared 60 feet above our heads on a floodlit balcony and, with several 'Oh, yeahs,' and several demonstrative tollings of his bell pronounced some completely unintelligible message. We all carried on drinking. Frank Smith wandered past, muttering darkly at this point that the assembled guests should have been piped in to dinner, but that the pipers had been dragged off into an adjacent garden for a photocall.

Nobody noticed the apparent lack of fluency in the arrangements and, undaunted, Dennis appeared again - this time at ground level – to declare 'Oh yeah. Your dinner is getting cold!' A great ad-lib that saved the day for Britain as we all trooped into a dining room as glittery as the guests now being seated.

Still in tow with the SEMA crew and reunited with Ian Topping (who now realised that I was not one of the SEMA crew), we took our places with our allocated hosts for the evening, two of the aforementioned ex-pats. We were also joined by a Gurkha... In conversation with Mr. and Mrs. Expat, it transpired that they were the latest members of the Monte Carlo club, having only been resident for a number of weeks. They had moved from their home in Switzerland – because it gets awfully cold in the winter. I sympathised.

They were a very friendly couple and thankfully knew next to nothing about the Manchester Bid, being recent additions to the circuit. They politely agreed that the Bid was a great idea for Manchester, they had been there once - many years ago - and had had a really good time. We didn't enquire how it compared with their last two abodes. Anyway, Mrs. Expat thought that our Lord Mayor, Bob Scott, was wonderful. So much so that she volunteered to help the working party conscripted to shift boxes to the press conference at eight the next morning. Mr. Expat declined and said he had no intention of seeing eight o'clock in the morning, let alone getting up and working.

As we ate I glanced around the room and noticed that Barry from Vision UK, who had driven the van full of print and display from Manchester, was seated next to Lord Jeffrey Archer. Maybe there was an element of the surreal about every table.

There were speeches from the great and the good – and John Gummer – before we said our goodbyes, gave thanks and teetered back to the Beach Plaza for three or four hours sleep before the working party assembled again at eight am.

A quick nightcap in the bar revealed the horticulturalists and their accompanying wives in deep and drunken conversation with a distinguished looking Australian gentleman. (I was unable to determine whether they had been to the reception or not.) As they got up to turn in my worst fears were again confirmed by one of the ample, bouffant-haired ladies saying with a slight slur, "I had another shoe somewhere...".

The distinguished Aussie joined in a more temperate conversation with our party and, on mutually questioning our reasons for being in Monte Carlo, it transpired that he was head of the Australian Bid Presentation Team. I guess with quickly exchanged glances between us Brits. that we mentally cancelled out 'Coronation Street' with 'Sylvania Waters.' Best not to try and put up a defence, I thought.

The sun rose before me and I made it for seven fifteen. A full pot of black coffee, croissants and a fag on the balcony and I was attired in Bid T-shirt and off to the Loews Hotel and the Manchester 2000 Press Office. Only a mile from my hotel, but a steady walk in that inflated early morning temperature finished me off before the really heavy work began.

And heavy it was. The entire contents of Barry's van had to be manhandled down several corridors into the goods lift and into the hotel service area, down a ramp and across a busy road into the Congress Hall for the press conference. I was in good company, rubbing sweaty shoulders with Chief Inspector Trevor Barton of the Greater Manchester police, who I had last met in his press office at Police HQ arranging for the bannering of that establishment.

The Bid Press Office itself was a hive of activity even at that early hour, with fax machines, telephones and photocopiers working relentlessly, demonstrating again the intensity of work involved in the Bid. The PR crew rarely emerged from this commandeered suite at the Loews Hotel for the entire three days.

The final stretch to the Congress Hall, impossibly heavy trolley in hand, was across the covered stretch of road by the Mediterranean that I had seen the greats of World motor racing tackling over many years in the Monaco Grand Prix. The traffic was travelling a little more sedately, but surely the greatest of indignities would have been to be killed by a Fiat Uno while pushing a trolley across a grand-prix circuit.

At the Congress Hall the same shifting routine had to be followed in reverse, with the press conference scheduled to be held at the same physical level that all of the material had been stored at originally, but in a different building. As long as they didn't want it all shifting back afterwards...

I retired defeated after three hours, my grey T-shirt now an overall darker shade of sweaty grey and wandered the mile back to the Beach

Plaza in the steadily growing heat. Looking onto the terrace of the hotel from my balcony, I could see the next reception in an advanced state of preparation. Tables, marquees and sun umbrellas covered the ground from my elevated viewpoint, with a small army of white shirted catering people flitting from the shade of one umbrella to the next, laying the silver service.

This time British Airways was flying the flag by picking up the tab. Just under an hour to go before all hands on deck for this particular do, so time for a shower, a cool down and the selection of suitable attire for this particular event – lightweight trousers, a Bid polo shirt and the panama hat seemed appropriate.

Wandering onto the terrace an hour later I was handed an unidentifiable cocktail by one of the dozens of waiters. It went down in one for refreshment value – but discreetly of course. The next four drinks followed in quick succession, but all were straight orange juice with ice to try and combat the soaring effect of midday temperatures. The kids were here and in full flight with steel band and choir, very soon livening up proceedings as more guests arrived. The noise of the guests making small talk, the sea and the seabirds, the kids, all made a spectacular patina of sound as I stood quietly to one side, observing. The partying intensified and the conga (Britain's traditional dance) broke out all over the terrace, involving the kids, various uniformed ranks of the police, the Coldstream Guards, Scottish pipers, a politician or two and Dennis the Town Cryer from Sandbach. Was this the reserved British that the world knew? Well not today obviously. This was the British in all their daily guises just having a good time and showing everybody else that they could have a good time – even if was only lunchtime.

In the corner of the terrace there were one or two tables under the cooling shade of the trees. I wandered over to continue my observation away from the baking heat and sat for half an hour or so watching with fascination and amusement. Shirley Bassey arrived, now a resident of Monte Carlo as is Ringo, who had apparently wandered from his apartment in the next block to the hotel. Someone said that Sean

Connery was at the party too. I didn't see him from my shaded but fixed vantage point, but I had no reason to doubt the fact.

Gradually the shade beckoned more of the guests and my haven was invaded by Bill Morgan, Chairman of CMDC, John Broome, the man who invented Alton Towers, Rob Green, the man who invented personal radar dishes, Barry from Vision UK, the man who had dinner with Jeffrey Archer and Dennis the Town Cryer from Sandbach. The table was completed by the company of a charming and very suave British expat, who, with absolutely no airs and graces at all, answered polite questions from one or two of the rest of us such as, "Why do you live here?" (Dumb question.) "Because I don't pay tax." And, "What kind of business are you in?" "Finance." "Oh, really, where is your company?" "Global." Conversation killer, eh?

Dennis, more concerned with the vital things in life, ate a good meal and three pieces of cake. Oh, yeah.

I stayed put as the assembly began to drift off a couple of hours later. Lyn Fenton sidled quietly up as the guests thinned and told me that I was included in the official party to go to the Sporting Club for the presentation to the IOC on the following morning. I had hoped to be there, but was nonetheless delighted to hear confirmation.

Half an hour more in the shade and everybody was gone apart from the odd personality here and there. I wandered across the terrace and back up to my room for a well earned half hour rest before the next gruelling assignment – assembly in the Casino Square to show support for the kids in their public performance and then on to the Monaco Yacht Club for cocktails. It was getting tougher all the time.

In Casino Square that afternoon, the youngsters from each of the bidding cities had been given a 45-minute slot to perform for their country. The Brits were due on at five and, arriving at four thirty, I caught the last half hour of 10 tiny and seemingly identical Chinese girls singing national songs for their country. They were charming and were given polite and studious attention by the crowds in the Square for the concert. But it was disconcerting in that they all looked identical – like Mikado peas in a pod – and smiled or waved at exactly the moments that it appeared that they had been drilled to do so. They all bowed in unison to the genuinely appreciative applause and tripped off the stage lightly in the wake of their choir mistress.

Five minutes later and Casino Square was pulsating to the sounds of the Wythenshawe and Levenshulme choir and steel band, giving the performance of their lives. The contrast to the Chinese girls could not have been greater, both in spirit and in looks. This marvellously multi-ethnic crowd, in jeans and trainers with as many earrings attached to the boys as the girls, gave it all they had and captured every nationality in the audience with their energy. And every nationality this time joined in their conga, with the 'Best of British' crowd supplanted by Australians, Germans in yellow Berlin Bid T-shirts, plus old and young alike from the rest of the crowd. They were simply terrific. And the presentation was hammed up perfectly by British self satire, when Queen Elizabeth the First arrived in full costume to gaze aloofly at the partying, accompanied by two pin-stripe suited and bowler hatted gentlemen carrying umbrellas, who jived stiffly to the pulsating music.

Despite every one of the assembled crowd shouting for more, the 45-minute slot had to be religiously stuck to and Casino Square was quiet once more, although, I suspect never to be quite the same again. I was talking to the kids and their bandana'd teacher afterwards and he told me that one of the Berlin supporters had come to him as the performance finished and, in reasonable English had said, "You know, Manchester can't lose." Maybe the meaning of the comment was more lateral than literal, but I knew exactly what she meant.

As the crowd cleared, Jim Chapman and I waited by the Casino steps to join up with the rest of the party to walk to the Yacht Club. I noticed that the square was suddenly filling up with heavily armed French CRS officers and barriers were being erected quietly but quickly. The Berlin team were due to make some sort of presentation and they were obviously preparing for more of the trouble that had dogged the German bid to date.

Bob Scott wandered out of the hotel on the square where he had been lobbying for almost a week non-stop. He looked tired and, I think, had just emerged for a breath of fresh air. Bob told Jim and me that he had secured 26 votes that he was sure of, plus a further six that he was unsure of. "I just feel though," he said, "that we've not done enough, not got to as many members as we should have." How ironic and prophetic these words were to become.

Suddenly, from amongst the Berlin crowd, there were shouts and scuffles. As the TV and CRS arrived simultaneously 20 feet away from where we were standing, Bob melted away instantly; Bob Scott on telly so close to an anti IOC demonstration from whatever country would be bad news for Britain at this late stage. Jim and I watched as demonstrators were dragged off by the police.

The Coldstream Guards Band was due to play in the Casino Square gardens in half an hour and so the now assembled party decided to arrive late at the Yacht Club and watch the beginning of the recital. Shortly after we learnt that the chairs the kids had been using were to double up for the Guard and so, in a rather undignified way, two or three of us picked up as many as we could carry and transported them to the gardens.

Not something that we were desperate to do, but in order to legitimately get to the site of the band performance we had to walk right between the position of the Berliners presenting their (very silly) yellow bear mascot to the German TV stations and those self same camera crews. Never ones to miss the chance of spoiling a good shot.

Band underway we walked down the steep harbour-side road and round the quay to the Monaco Yacht Club. Now at this point I have to explain that my previous understanding of 'yacht' and the meaning of 'yacht' in that particular part of the world are somewhat different. As we stood at the Club, we craned our necks upwards to smile back at the crews of said yachts who were gazing down on us in an uninterested way. They'd seen it all before – probably last night and the night before and...

We weren't impressed by it all, of course not. Dennis was there. An hour and one or two cocktails later, James Froomberg, Senior Partner of KPMG London, wandered over to say hello and tell me that everyone was well aware of what Drawing Board had done for the Bid. He was, to put it politely, out of his accountant's tree, but the comment was completely unprompted and I can only look upon it as genuine.

We were to meet up with James in the early hours of the next morning, with the interim period for our small gathering being spent eating, to soak up the seemingly innocuous but deadly cocktails, while he assured us that this was a continuous consumption for him since the lunchtime reception and he had no need of food.

And so back into town to find a restaurant. The party for the meal consisted of Frank Smith, Vin Sumner, Janet Harrison, Liz Jeffreys – Chief Executive of GMVCB – and myself. The hill which we had ambled down two or three hours earlier seemed much more daunting looking back up at it, especially when Frank informed us that the restaurant he had in mind was so far up the hill that it was actually just over the border of the Principality (although still in the town) and was therefore France rather than Monaco.

Then, perpetuating the dream, the Bid's red Rolls Royce appeared on the quayside driving towards us. Frank deftly flagged the limousine down and the chauffeur's window descended silently as it stopped beside us. "Give us a lift up to town," requested Frank. The Chauffeur replied, "Sorry, its' now five to nine. I'm on my way to pick up Steve Redgrave and Tara told me that if I wasn't there at exactly nine o'clock she'd cut off part of my anatomy – and she didn't mean my hands." The window rose again as the car slid off along the quayside by the glistening yachts.

But we were saved. Just another hundred yards on our hike and one of the specially imported British black cabs pulled up just ahead of us. Although these vehicles were not for hire and were just to have a British presence on the streets of Monte Carlo, the cabbie agreed to take us to the restaurant and so it was that we arrived at the door of an Italian restaurant, over the Monaco border and in France (but still in Monte Carlo), in a Manchester black cab five minutes later.

The restaurateur asked if we would like to sit on the terrace. This seemed like a good idea, but we were perplexed for a minute or two as he sat us at a table in a back room. It was only when we looked up at the ceiling some four storeys above us did we deduce that the deep blue starry sky painting was actually the Mediterranean sky.

The restaurant terrace had an electric retractable roof. It soon transpired that the gadgetry was not limited to just the roof; Liz went to the loo and reappeared a couple of minutes later in fits of laughter. Unable to tell us through the giggles what had tickled her, Janet disappeared to investigate and returned in a similar state. When the girls had regained their composure, they managed to explain that when the electronic button was pressed to flush the loo, the toilet seat disappeared into the back of the cistern and a new seat folded down from the front of the cistern to replace it. Hygiene taken to extremes, I think.

Vin and I could not resist a look at this particular gizmo and so we ventured into the ladies at a quiet moment. Expectantly we pressed the button. The loo flushed but the seat stayed where it was. We were puzzled. But then the inspiration came to sit on the seat before flushing it. Eureka! Not only was the toilet seat ingenious, it was also smart-arse enough to recognise when it had been sat on and when it was being fooled.

Meal over, we wandered back into Monte Carlo to find Flashman's. Yes, you've guessed it. Even Monte Carlo has an English pub. But tonight Flashman's was slightly different – they were serving free Boddington's Bitter, shipped in especially by the brewery to support the Bid.

Manchester really had taken over Monte Carlo for the week. An hour later and an hour worse for wear, Janet, Vin and myself took a cab back to the hotel and, gluttons for punishment as is often the case after a drink or two too many, we resolved to take a night-cap by the pool.

It was here that we re-encountered the indomitable and now even more extremely pissed Senior Partner of KPMG.

He had somehow taken up company with the Australian Channel 9 TV crew and, although we were not quite sure in what manner he had engaged them in conversation, James was by this time berating them for being sons of deported British criminals, cultureless, pretentious, inferior cousins of decent English stock and generally not at all a nice race of people.

The Aussies, recognising the condition he was in, were taking it all in good part and, it has to be said, giving James back as much as he was dishing out, but in a more amused manner. Finally, the biggest, beefiest and most sun-tanned of the Channel 9 crew said to James that the Brits were incapable of winning anything. For James, in his emotional state, this was the last straw.

Despite our trying to tell James that he would surely kill himself, he already had his trousers undone and had challenged Mr. Muscles to four lengths of the pool. There was a moment of incredulity from the Australians as James stood by the pool trouserless, still wearing shirt and tie, plus specs and of course still with both socks on. The Aussie couldn't resist it. As James stripped down to his M & S Y-fronts, the TV man stripped down to sun-tan and boxer shorts. Somebody shouted 'Go' and they did.

Thirteen stones of tightly honed flesh thrashed through the water at what, to me, was an amazing pace. But...ten stones of (white) skin and bones slid through the water with hardly a ripple and at the speed of an Exocet missile.

By the beginning of the final length, James was so far ahead that he executed the coup de grace. He turned gracefully over and swam the last leg in an exaggerated leisurely back- stroke. One of the most wonderfully funny and triumphant moments of British sport I have ever witnessed.

James was standing on the side of the pool already reaching for another drink as the defeated Aussie hauled himself panting, out of the pool. "Baaastard," he said.

That night the whole of Monte Carlo was woken and then kept awake by the most ferocious thunderstorm I have ever cowered under. I am sure that every delegate, connected with every bid, thought – if only fleetingly – that the Gods were rousing themselves for the momentous decisions to be taken later that day.

Eight o'clock and we were on the streets at the gates of the Sporting Club with the kids from the band, waving Union Jacks as the IOC delegates entered for day four of the one-hundred-and-first IOC Session. The torrential rain was to last through the day and night of September 23rd. It was, we all agreed, an omen. But which way?

One of the limousines slowed as it drew level with us and the rear window slid down. It was Princess Anne and she smiled at the kids with genuine warmth. The only other major presence at the gates of the Sporting Club were the Berliners. One particularly nutty German decided that he could compete with the kids' chanting of 'Manchester, Manchester,' but his good natured shouting for 'Berlin' was no competition to bubbling enthusiasm in the rain. The time had come. We showered the Mediterranean rain away and donned our British Bid uniforms of blue blazers, grey trousers, white shirts, Bid ties and Panama hats before reconvening in the lobby of the hotel.

As I entered the lift on the sixth floor I was aware of six or seven people standing in silence facing me. I accompanied them in silence for a few seconds as I realised that they were all members of the Sydney Bid

Team in their own corporate uniforms. The doors of the lift slid quietly shut behind me. There was a further silence as we surveyed each other apprehensively and then a voice from the back drawled, "Welcome to Austraaalia."

From the lobby of the Beach Plaza a cab took us to the lobby of the Loews where we were all to convene at 10 o'clock. The main players were already there and the tension they were feeling soon transferred itself to us. There was polite, if strained conversation as we all ruminated on the years that everyone had toiled so hard on the Bid just preparing for this day. People drifted around quietly and talked in hushed voices. Someone spoke to me and I joined in with small talk. It was Jeffrey Archer. It was the only moment I was ever going to have to tell him that I thought his books were crap. I didn't. He drifted off.

As the Scottish pipers began their banshee fanfare the TV lights kicked up and we moved out to get on to the Manchester 2000 coach. Norma Charlton sat beside me and we continued the nervous small talk on the journey to the Sporting Club, arriving at the gates in the rain to be greeted by the marvellous kids still waving their sodden Union Jacks and chanting 'Manchester, Manchester.'

The security cordon closed behind the coach and I mentioned to Norma that in the early hours of that morning, standing on the balcony of the hotel watching the storm, I had seen a gun-boat slide quietly out of view behind the headland that the Sporting Club occupied. All this for the Games. All this for the IOC.

As we left the coach we were ushered under the shelter of a terrace at the Club, to wait for the Australian delegation to emerge from their presentation. I looked around at our bevy of politicians, personalities and sports stars sheltering from the rain, accompanied by pipers and a trio of fanfare trumpeters from the Coldstream Guards in ceremonial dress. It was an impressive collection of the 'Best of British.' As the Australian contingent walked by us on the way out we spotted Joan Sutherland in their midst. Some anonymous British wag from amongst our party shouted, "Is that the best you can do?"

As we filed in to take our places it felt like a mass interview for the job you really wanted to get. The stomach muscles were beginning to tense – and would stay that way for the next seven or eight hours. Tanni Gray had to be carried into the Sporting Club in her wheelchair – no disabled access here. A strange contradiction for a presentation aimed at people who cared for 'Sport for all.'

The auditorium resembled the hall of the United Nations, with each delegate seated at a desk in concentric curved sweeps, with headphones for translations and microphones for questions. The hall was darkened as Samaranch made his introduction and the Manchester Olympic Bid Presentation began with Janet's film. Sitting next to her, I felt that she was shaking with tension. Months of work had gone into these four minutes that had to grab the IOC and hook them for the rest of the presentation. I held on to her arm to try and help, but I was probably shaking just as much.

The film was terrific and I will always try to keep a copy with this diary of the days, because it seemed somehow to sum up what we all desperately wanted for the City and how we had all worked.

The rest of the 40-minute presentation was good – and we learned later that the other bidding cities were genuinely impressed. There were one or two more short films, interspersed with Bob Scott and John Major making the case for Manchester as strongly as I think it could have been put. The whole presentation, but particularly the film, was an emotional experience. Without being there it is impossible to describe the circumstances or the feelings generated by years of work culminated in a 40-minute presentation. Many of the hard bitten Bid team there were on the verge of tears. Some couldn't hold it back, including one notable Chief Inspector from Greater Manchester Police.

As the presentation finished we burst into spontaneous applause, before Samaranch gave his thanks and we filed out. I said to someone,

"That was a terrific presentation," and got the worldly reply, "Yes, but were they listening?"

Back at the Loews we crossed the Congress Hall for a packed press conference. Although the knot in the stomach was still there, there was a recognisable feeling of relief that the presentation had gone well and according to plan. Apart from fielding technical questions Bob expressed that now the work was over, whatever the outcome we had played our best shots. I don't think that it was a sense of achievement, but more a sense of relief that prompted the reply from Bob when asked how he felt... "I'm reet chuffed."

The waiting game now began, with seven hours before we were to assemble in the stadium for the decision. We took a cab back to the Beach Plaza to watch the other presentations on closed circuit television. Back at the hotel members of the other bidding cities had assembled in the bar to do the same. There was a proliferation of Australians and the sense of relief felt by all was reflected in the humour and friendship now being shown. The inter-continental satire was at its sharpest – and everyone confessed to the same knotted stomach.

As the Beijing presentation began on CCTV in the hotel, something of the satire went out of the comments and the true feelings towards the Chinese bid from everyone there became evident. Whoever won, whoever lost, we had to stop the Chinese from making a mockery of the Games and more importantly, of human rights.

The hours drifted on and people drifted in and out of the bar. I was watched with great amusement by a small multi-national gathering a few feet away, as a middle-aged lady from Istanbul who had, for some reason not got accreditation for the evening, somehow perceived that I could get her in there and hinted that she would accompany me. I am still not sure what she had in mind but my theory seemed to be in line with the onlookers. I retired a few feet to the company of two landlords from Boddington pubs in Manchester, who had apparently won a brewery competition to be in Monte Carlo for the decision. They did not have a clue what was going on and had apparently just been given air tickets and a hotel voucher - not a great way to reward people for winning a competition. I had a drink with them and explained the processes that were happening on the lead-up to the announcement that evening. I think they were grateful that somebody had taken the trouble to try and explain things to them and I was grateful that they had provided a haven from the lady from Istanbul. I was glad of their company again in the early hours of the following morning.

At five o'clock we made our way to the Louis II stadium. It was far too early, but we had had long enough sitting aimlessly in one place and so decided to go and sit aimlessly somewhere else. Preparations were being made to broadcast the decision world-wide and we sat and watched in the absence of alternative amusement. The time dragged and the tension grew by the minute. Every delegate from every city must have been going through the same see-saw of believing one minute and then dismissing the idea as being impossible the next. Patriotic singing broke out – the best of all tension relievers. We took our turn with 'Land of Hope and Glory,' which didn't seem somehow as appropriate as 'Waltzing Matilda' from the Aussies or unintelligible dirges from the Turks and Chinese. The assembled delegates became quiet again.

Somehow at that point I knew all was lost. I took out my invitation and wrote on it, 'Too much of a dream. Monte Carlo. 6.15pm. September 23rd, 1993.' I don't know why I did it, but it made me very depressed. I think it was a case of whether the see-saw was up or down in the moments before the presentation began. I was on the seat touching the ground, looking up at the adversaries. I hadn't noticed, but Janet was next to me on the see-saw. She had her head down and was crying quietly. Cramming so much emotion into a few hours had affected everyone and, not for the first time, I knew that anyone who was not there, would not be able to understand. As the presentation was about to begin with a choreographed show, everyone shook hands as though we were embarking on something that could mean we would never see each other again. But maybe it was just that we would never see each other again in the same extraordinary circumstances of mind. Whichever way it went, life would never be the same.

The dance show was truly spectacular and would have been enormously enjoyable apart from the circumstances. I suppose that something was needed to make the evening an event for those assembled who were not completely partisan to one cause or another. They showed the scenes back home in the bidding cities by satellite. The sight of the Castlefield Basin brought a feeling of wonder and strange responsibility. When we had left Manchester, one of our greatest enemies had seemed the indifference of a large population of not only our city, but the country. I had phoned back home a couple of times and treated with a little scepticism the reports that suddenly everyone was believing what we had been trying to make them believe for years. It might just be possible...although it might just be too much of a dream.

Seven fifteen arrived. Samaranch arrived. The IOC arrived and filed in to almost complete silence. As the voting adjudicators filed on to the stage beside Samaranch, Kevin Gosper, IOC member for Australia and assistant to Samaranch, could barely disguise a smile. Or was I imagining it? Samaranch went through the list of thanks to the bidding cities again and then said, "The host city for the 2000 Olympic Games will be..." hour upon hour to open the envelope as the stomach knotted to its furthest extent before bursting, "Sydney."

Beside us the Australians erupted in that vortex of sound that we had talked about earlier in the day. "I just want to scream Yes! And jump out of my seat like we saw the Atlanta team do last time. I just want to be part of that moment," Janet had said. We knew exactly what she meant.

We sat in silence as the party beside us fell into screaming, shouting chaos.

"What will Bob do now?" I asked myself out loud.

As the stomach settled into an equally intense but totally different experience, I joined in the fringe of the celebration and shook some Australian hands, gave some words of congratulation. At close hand there were tears in every eye visible. To the right there was elation - to the left, desperate disappointment.

At the moment of the decision, as the Australians had erupted in celebration, a koala bear Sydney mascot had flown 30 feet into the air and landed on my knee. I clipped the bear on to my red, white and blue hat-band as we stood up to leave. Nobody had told us what happened if we lost. There was no reason to stay; Samaranch had apparently been planning to make a speech, but this was abandoned in the face of wild celebrations from the Australians.

We stood up and filed out past the party, shoulder to shoulder with Turks, Germans and Chinese – all as silent as ourselves.

At least China had not won.

Drifting back to the Loews, we gathered for a final reception. Nobody joked about it being the last supper, but I am sure that the thought occurred to us all. As people assembled quietly and stood around in groups, I took a beer from one of the silver trays being wielded skilfully around the room by dickie-bowed waiters. The champagne being offered on the same trays seemed a little flat. Sitting observing the guests assemble, as I had done in different circumstances the day before, I exchanged a few words with Frank and Lyn Fenton, who were greeting people as they arrived.

 The status of the players now counted for nothing as each and every arrival was greeted with a mutual hug and very few words. Princess Anne arrived. She had not been specifically invited or expected to join the group for supper and she came in as just another one of the team. It was that kind of occasion.

After drinks we were ushered into a room where we were to eat. I sat with Jim Chapman, James Burland, the stadium architect, most of the team from AMEC and Terry Thomas, Chairman of the Co-Op Bank. Jim Ramsbottom, Manchester's most notorious bookie and sometime property developer, completed the table. This particular rough and genuine diamond instantly lifted the atmosphere by loudly proposing a toast to "Manchester." We all stood and loudly concurred with the first of many glasses of wine. Immediately earmarked as the rowdiest table of the night, we did not, I fear, disappoint.

The concensus of conversation – based on no firm premise – was that we must get the stadium built. I suppose having the architect, the potential developers and the Chairman of the development committee on the table in the ample shape of Terry, as a group it was the only one that could ultimately achieve this particular goal.

A fine supper went down well, accompanied by probably as much alcohol as we could have consumed had we won. Jim Ramsbottom suddenly raised the tempo of the evening again as he startled us all by thumping the table and shouting, "We want Bob!" The chorus was taken up by everybody within a few seconds and, after a tumultuous minute or so, Sir David, Bob's father, stood up to tell us that his son was completing a round of interviews for the British media and would be along soon. Five minutes later, the whole room rose spontaneously to its feet as Bob Scott came in. The welcome could not have been greater had we been taking the Games home with us – a great tribute to the man who had instigated the whole idea and, despite his bluff, ebullient and sometimes almost bullying methods of management, had maintained the respect of everyone throughout the years. Standing on a chair to speak, Bob was immediately up-staged by his mum, who leapt to her feet as quickly as her age would allow, to straighten his jacket. The spontaneous cheers this time were for Mrs. Scott, rather than Bob.

As always, his words were eloquent and while I cannot recall the detail, his final statement in isolation might appear a little crass taken out of the emotion of the evening: he simply said, "We have won," and with those three words brought the house down.

The choir made a fantastically timely reappearance and sang a beautiful, quiet anthem of reflection, the title and words of which I cannot remember, followed by the British National anthem – 'Always look on the bright side of life, doo, doo...' And Princess Anne joined in. The whole event could not have been rehearsed or stage managed better – and it was all completely spontaneous.

A gloom descended on me and I felt a desperate need to leave the masses and reflect a little on my own for a while. I headed out of the hotel and down towards the glittering harbour. Unabated, the rain continued to pour down as I hunched under my Panama, Bid uniform becoming completely sodden in minutes.

I think that I would have carried on walking in one direction for an hour or so had I not, by the harbour, taken off my hat which was now so wet as to be useless at any kind of protection from the elements. I was horrified...the koala was gone! I don't know why, but I turned round to retrace my steps in the pouring rain, scouring the gutters for a two inch bear. After about a mile I spotted a small object on the pavement ahead. No, I couldn't be that lucky! My joy was probably a reflection of the current warped state of mind, but I clipped him back into place and decided it was time to go back to the hotel. Walking back through Casino Square my eye was caught by a furtive figure dodging cars and hanging baskets in a slightly hunched manner. As the figure passed by a lit window, I recognised Graham Stringer, the leader of our City Council. My eye followed him as he darted into a bar, where I noticed Margaret Nuttall, Bill Enevoldson and one or two of the team gathered around a table on the pavement, just under the shelter of an awning. I crossed the road and refused their invitation to join them, saying I was off back to the hotel (with my bear) to have a drink with the Aussies.

Back at the hotel half an hour later, I went up to my room, took a quick shower and donned Bid T-shirt and jeans, before going back down to the bar. During the course of a couple more beers, one or two more of our crew arrived in from the rain. Yet again I was drinking with Janet and Vin. This time Stuart Greaves from Mainstream accompanied us. We were joined by a chap who was some sort of marketing consultant to Boddingtons. His name thankfully escapes me, but I soon realised that he was the 'prat' whom everyone had been talking about for the last day or so who was refusing to wear anything to do with the Bid.

His opening gambit was a mistake, particularly in the frame of mind I was in at the time. "We should never have Bid in the first place unless we were going to do it properly." My eyes, I am sure, came even further out of my head than before, due to alcohol consumption. From someone who had patently been there on a complete jolly and made no contribution to the effort I found this very hard to take. I questioned him politely on what the premise of his argument was and he seemed to be telling me that nobody had done anything other than Boddingtons. At this point I had to point out that in my opinion, Boddingtons had done sod all apart from stick the logo on their TV ads and a few million cans.

"Ah," he replied, "but what has the Bid done for the deprived kids of Manchester?" Now I can take most things, but pseudo-socialism really gets my goat, particularly when I'm drunk and have spent a proportion of the evening wandering around in the rain looking for a toy koala bear. I asked Mr. Boddington whether he had been lying in his comfy bed that morning, paid for – no doubt – by somebody else, while I was on the streets of Monte Carlo in the rain with exactly those kids he was talking about.

The following exchanges are a blur, but I do remember (and drunk as I was, it struck me as amusing at the time) I accused him of not putting forward a single intellectual argument and then within seconds told him he was "talking bollocks." He strutted off and came back five minutes later to apologise. I remember saying that I wasn't accepting an apology from a prat like him and at this point embroiled my two Boddington landlord friends into the row, whom I thankfully bought a drink for earlier on in the day.

From here I was on safe ground, because I knew that they had an axe to grind about the brewery and anyway it now meant that there were three of us and one of him.

At this point I was vaguely aware of my companions deciding that it was time we adjourned to a hotel room and drink from the mini-bar in safety. It seemed like a good idea. We fell into the lift. In one corner was a very large male Australian, who was singing to himself very quietly:

> "I don't care if it rains or freezes,
> I am safe in the hands of Jesus.
> I am Jesus' little lamb,
> Yes, by Jesus Christ I am."

Somehow we all ended up in the room of this Antipodean - a journalist. I am not sure exactly how, but I do remember the room. It resembled the worst kind of student flat I had ever seen in my life. The floor was littered with old newspapers, dirty washing and bottles – some empty, some part-full – of every alcoholic kind.

Feeling that I should make some sort of contribution to the beverage supply I staggered to my room to raid the mini-bar. Luckily we were on the same floor, otherwise I think that the task might have defeated me. On the way back I bumped into Matthew (literally) who had spent half of the last four days sweltering inside a silly Manchester Lion costume. I informed him of our find and asked where Johnathan was (who had spent the rest of the four days in the costume), so he would not miss the treat. Apparently Johnathan was inside their room, apparently so soundly asleep that Matt had been hammering on the door attempting to get in for the past half hour. He was just returning with a spare key from the lobby.

We set off to collect Johnathan and, entering the room, discovered that he was, as suspected, dead to the world. Our every attempt to wake him – mainly by shouting excessively straight into his ear – failed. And so we did the next best thing; we put a Union Jack hat on his head and a similar flag in his hand and left him to sleep it off. (Apparently he woke up in exactly the same position the following morning and presumed he had returned from the revelry of the night before wearing the hat and carrying the flag.)

Returning to the Aussie's room we settled in for a further drinking session which proved very easy. There was no need to move, you just picked up the nearest half empty bottle from the floor. After a while we decided that we should introduce ourselves by name. We goggled when he told us his name was Bruce – nobody from Australia is really called Bruce. But he picked up a random fax from the floor to prove the fact; it was addressed to Bruce Wilson. His humour and intelligence were paramount, regaling us with stories of his four marriages, his journalistic travels and the Australian attitude to Britain and 'Her Maj.' He was a combination of Paul Hogan and Barry Humphries and we just sat and listened to his tales until he became too drunk to talk. Or maybe we were too drunk to listen... Dawn was approaching and we retired.

I missed breakfast.

Assembling at 10 the same morning, the British contingent was subdued, reflecting on the tragedy of the previous evening. We said our goodbyes to the vanquished Channel 9 swimmer, one or two Germans and I took a piece of paper from the barman with his address on it, so that I could send him some programmes from Manchester United.

At the airport we sat with Bobby and Norma Charlton, drinking black coffee and waiting for our flight. Trying to analyse the events of the night before, Bobby confirmed what Bob Scott had said to us on the Wednesday evening: 26 IOC members had sought him out, shook his hand and told him that Manchester had their vote. To finish up with only 11 votes was the most distressing thing of all. It meant that 15 of the IOC members had been lying when they said we had their vote. The question was - which 15? Or was it just that Beijing had looked so strong that these votes were switched to counter the Chinese cause? Maybe all will come out in time, maybe not.

The flight home was subdued, with a little half-hearted singing from some of the party. But the ebullience of the previous three days was gone. Bob made another thank you speech as we taxied to the terminal at Manchester. He thanked everyone for their efforts and said he wasn't just saying that because he was looking for a job now. As we came into the arrivals hall, a phalanx of TV and press were waiting for Bob. Everyone waiting for the arrival of friends and relatives cheered spontaneously as they spotted Bob leading the team into the hall. Some measure of how the Bid had finally captured the imagination of the City. As we walked out, Bob was swamped by the media. I walked through and out of the doors to find a cab. I had to pick the kids up at five.

After these heady days life got back to normal. Well, as normal as it ever was. I had itchy feet again and, as part of putting together the Bid Document and therefore the first master plan for Manchester I began to look around. There was an area that I had always known as Knott Mill. If you can remember the ads. for 'Knott Mill Carpets', then you are at least as old as I am. In the document it was boldly called the City Southern Gateway. I may have made that one up too. I can't remember. It was called this because it was trapped between two main routes into the city: Princess Parkway and Chester Road.

Now nothing happened between these routes as they entered the city. The area was basically full of industrial sheds (of a very low quality) and old mill buildings (of a high quality, but derelict). We had a slight diversion when Tony's Factory Records went bust and had the notion that we could buy the offices to move into. I wandered round the building with Tony as he reminisced about the cost of slightly pink tinged plaster at 10 times the cost of normal plaster and the airport landing light on the roof. Expensive, useless, but 'situationist.' I heard all this again only in the last couple of years when, after Tony's death, I could bring myself to watch '24 Hour Party People.' But we were outbid and so back to wandering round City Southern Gateway.

I knew a young urban developer called Nick Johnson and to be quite honest wasn't sure how we'd met. But Nick had just set up Nick Johnson Urban Development and, I think, I was one of his first clients. Nick wandered round all of these often derelict buildings with me and ultimately negotiated the purchase of a mill at 4 Jordan Street: 10,000 square feet, desperately in need of lots of TLC and a big splodge of money for refurbishment.

So off I went to the bank again, outstanding liabilities on 44 Canal Street sorted out and some left over to fund the purchase of the building, if not the refurbishment. The bank manager flinched when I told him about my scheme. But he agreed to stump up the necessary and the deal was on. I had met and admired Roger Stephenson and Jeff Bell (Stephenson Bell) some years before and had even said to Rog that I wanted to work with him one day.

Of course I asked him and his team to regenerate 4 Jordan Street, originally a Victorian textile warehouse. Right up Rog's street. Well, ours actually. And when he showed me his first scheme, which was also the one we went with, he also said that he was looking for premises for a period of about a year and would we lease him the top floor when the work was done. Now we, as a business, could never have filled the space. We were never that big and anyway the whole idea had also been to generate income from other creative industry tenants.

There then ensued nine months of mayhem. Despite every stage being thoroughly planned the refurbishment was inevitably delivered late. On budget, but late. Well that's half the battle. The Stephenson Bell scheme looked great. The building we moved into was, frankly, a building site. But all settled down eventually and those weeks and probably months working with hard hats on are very much an insignificant blip in the past now.

And talking of time scales, Rog, Jeff and their team stayed for seven years.

Happily, 4 Jordan Street drew a lot of attention and was featured in the Architect's Journal and other publications, notably, perhaps, as the main feature in Central Manchester Development Corporation's annual review. It was cited as a 'Prime example of how Manchester could be rejuvenated by good design and investment.'

Now I had worked with John Glester, the CEO of CMDC, for several years including on the Olympic Bid. First, I had applied to CMDC for a grant to help with refurbishment and been refused. Second, they hadn't even asked me if they could feature the building in all its glory. So I phoned John and had a bit of banter. I've not seen him for years, but I wonder if he's still got 'I'm forever blowing bubbles' as the ring tone on his phone?

The consolation prize for the Manchester for not winning the Olympic Games was to be asked to 'bid' for the Commonwealth Games. Now it was never admitted, but bidding was a bit of a rich phrase for this. I am sure that because of all the efforts, planning and infrastructure that was starting to happen in the city we were – ahem - pretty sure to get the Commonwealth Games.

A bid was put in, the marketing collaterals of which were created by my old friends at Creative Lynx. Celebration! We – the City of Manchester - was awarded the Games for 2002. In the time scale that these things operate to I guess that this was about 1995. I will have a record somewhere, but it's not significant. But the imagery, the brand for the Games, still had to be developed. I had learnt during our work on the Olympic Bid that the imagery for a bid is completely different to that for the event – or another major sporting event – itself.

It might be worth going back a little to the stick that we – as designers – and the City got for the brand created for the Olympic Bid. It featured patriotic blue flames and a giant hint of the Union Flag. We were criticised for being corny and jingoistic with our imagery and this stretched, for example, to some of the films prepared to support the Bid. These films featured the Coldstream Guards, the Queen and lots of 'Green and Pleasant Land.' (But no 'Dark Satanic Mills.') Target markets.

Very early on Bob had said to me that we were bidding for support from

IOC members all over the world. They came from massively different backgrounds, some of them third world and certainly a lot from the Far East. "Don't ever presume that people know where England is, let alone Manchester." Therefore, we started every global communication by zooming in first on Europe, then Britain, then England, then Manchester. And in the marcomms we gave them what they would expect in order to relate to us as a city and a country. If we had done something very trendy and Madchester – which is what we were criticised for not doing – it would have been lost on the IOC members.

Same goes for the Commonwealth Games. The bid needs to look different from the event. And so (déjà vu) we were asked to pitch for the job once the Games was secured. It was a bit bizarre, because we were pitching to the same people we had worked with for years on the Olympic Bid – apart from Bob Scott, who had gone off to mastermind London's Bid for the 2012 Olympics which of course he won, along with a Knighthood. Deservedly.

That team was Mike Dyble, Fran Toms and Penny Boothman amongst others. The pitch was against several other design groups from Manchester and nationally, although the original MDC was no longer on the scene in the same guise as in the late 80's. A young designer called Mark Bottomley was responsible for the concept of our pitch. And it has to be said that things were a bit fraught leading up to pitch day. We won. I heard later that some of the 'pitchers' said it was fixed, which it wasn't and that did hurt me. But we also beat a pitch from Identica – the company now run by Michael Peters whom I had admired and groupied many, many years before. That was satisfying. We also won the fee, which just about covered the design time we had spent. That was an improvement on 1988! Although we had to assign the copyright for a quid. Fair enough but we never got the quid.

The account was handled by Rob Wyer, who has since gone on to run his own businesses successfully. Rob brought in the Marconi account to Drawing Board, which he worked on and was very lucrative for many years. I usually say that it was Rob and not the Directors of Marconi who was responsible for the incredible demise of that particular great British institution, because it coincided ultimately with the share price going from 15 quid to 15 pence.

Rob and Mark worked together very well for a short period after the account was awarded, but both left within the year to 'pursue other interests.' Anyway, we just got on with it and a newcomer to the business Helen Plumtree took charge of the account. (I was working in the States with Helen some years later and they insisted on calling her Miss Palmtree for some reason. Even sillier than her real name.)

So, names and pack drill. To be honest I only had an overseeing job on this one. It was a great one to do and I kept a close eye on it – mainly to arbitrate the rows – but was commercial, rather than driven by passion. My drive on the Olympic Bid was to contribute a little to the regeneration of my City. This was now starting to happen all around us and that was exciting to see. There is a lot that I could write about the process of delivering the Commonwealth Games brand, but I can't for propriety. I will record a few things.

A Games Marketing Director was appointed called Tony Hill. Tony has now gone on to become the Director of the Mancheser Musuem of Science and Industry. He was a bit of a rum bugger at times during our tenure of the account. Propriety. I can't publish the pictures, though I still have them Tony. Beware! But we worked well with Tony who was under a lot of pressure to deliver and to deliver under budget. Fair enough I guess, but it does add pressures.

I will cite one instance. We were asked to investigate and plan the creation of a sculpture as a permanent legacy to the City. It was to be based on the brand we had created. We had long been fans of a young London sculptress called Sophie Marsham. We went through the whole process and Sophie even made a quarter size maquette of the proposed sculpture, which was to be four metres high. The figures involved aren't relevant, but original art doesn't come cheap. This went on forever until eventually we got a message back from the City asking us to ask Sophie how much a three metre high one would be. I was too embarrassed to ask her.

Now I still had Cobi very firmly in my mind from 1992. I argued that the brand created was one thing, but the legacy a Cobiesque mascot could leave would be far greater. And when I say I argued, I mean argued. I lived in dread of a 'Mr. Blobby' mascot emerging. I had worked for many years with the most talented of illustrators, David Hughes. I discussed this with David and he was, of course, instantly fired up.

So off he went into Purdah for several weeks, before returning to the office with a shoe box. The shoe box had holes punched into it all over. Ever so carefully he took out a plasticine model. It was a baby lion. Well, maybe a juvenile lion. Well, maybe just a lion. It had a tattered ear and one eye. Yes, Cobiesque, but so individual in its own way. David had also done shedloads of drawings, showing how animated this character could be. He also produced the lion cub's life story. He also called the lion cub Kit.

Dave went on one about how the lion's mother and father had escaped from Belle Vue Zoo in the 1960s (which is when the Zoo closed down, I think. Yes, there used to be a Zoo – and roller coaster park - in Manchester). They had hidden in the disused mines under Bradford Gas Works, which used to be a colliery and was where the foundations of the City of Manchester Stadium were being laid. ("This bit's really run down. How about putting a stadium there…") And Kit was the grandchild (grand-cub) of those escapees. Dave had not only written Kit's life story he, of course, believed every one of his own words. It was wonderful and as he finally left the office after hours of waxing lyrical he carefully put the plasticine model back in the shoe box. "Dave," I asked, "Why has the box got holes in it?" He looked at me incredulously and said, "So he can breathe."

There then ensued the most tortuous of processes trying to convince the Commonwealth Games team that this was not only a great idea, it was more important than the brand. To be honest Tony Hill was for it, although constrained by 'the powers that be.' But we had such plans for Kit. He was to be a Big Issue salesman. He was to be a cheeky Manc, he was to be a musician. He was to be a businessman. He wasn't real (sorry Dave), he could be anything. Dave did masses of work on developing Kit and exploring ideas. He even produced a series of cards to give out to school kids, with Kit giving ideas on how to make up excuses to avoid games. Cheeky, Manc and would have been around still as our heritage if he had actually been born. Now apart from many, many people both in the City and within the Commonwealth Games team not really understanding Kit and the concept, Dave quite rightly dug his heels in about copyright and potential merchandising. And thereby lay the problem and the ultimate end of Kit before he had begun.

No agreement could be reached to pay Dave for a percentage of merchandising sales, which I am convinced would have been enormous and probably still going on today. The meetings were endless and excruciating, with Dave even refusing to leave experimental drawings with the Games team because he was so suspicious. I tried to mediate between the two parties, but didn't really get far. I was the one who had wanted Kit (although I knew not what our mascot would be when I started the process) and so I fought. But I guess I understood that the City and powers that be didn't really grasp the concept of David potentially getting a large financial reward for his idea.

Dave being Dave set to with a pencil after each meeting and angrily drew the proponents with Kit in the middle somewhere. These were hugely entertaining and I have them to this day somewhere. When it appeared that all was going to be lost I asked Tony Wilson to intervene – maybe on the basis that he could rant better than me. Tony had absolutely loved Kit right from the start. But then he could, of course, see the abstract, see potential. That was what Tony was. Further meetings ensued, this time involving Tony and the powers that be, but always – as always – with Yvette Livesey quietly overseeing and listening. Often catching my eye with the lightest of smiles as Tony and Dave both kicked off at the same time - which they usually did. Kit eventually fell by the wayside because agreement could not be reached and Dave, some weeks later, came back to see me with a whole wad of drawings.

He said that he was going to do a book about Kit and the whole process and how nobody understood and how they expected him to give the idea away for nothing and how nobody, nobody was going to cheapen his art and…. The drawings were wonderful and when we came to the section with drawings of meetings involving Tony and Yvette, David growled, "…and I'm going to call the book 'My Little Tony.'" Kit would have loved that, so would have Tony, although Dave never did produce the book.

Now this rankled with me enormously as you would expect. We carried on working on the marketing collaterals for the Games, with Helen Plumtree first in the line of fire for servicing the account. A full corporate identity manual was produced, along with all the other items necessary to make the brand cohesive. Tony Hill battled on under some adversity of budgets amidst constant querying of costs and invoices, which I can understand. The Games had to be delivered on budget, but it was difficult to provide a service when it was difficult to get the fees to do so. There was a feeling at Games HQ – no, more than a feeling – that we should be doing the work gratis, for the sake of the City. Now apart from the fact I had already spent many, many years putting in a huge amount of time gratis (none of my time on the Technical

Bid Document was invoiced, for example), we were a small company and just couldn't afford to do so. But anyway we ploughed on and, for example, developed the symbols for all of the individual events at the Games.

This had a quite amusing scenario attached to it a couple of years later, just before the Games themselves. Well I found it amusing. I had a call from Tony Hill. He was a bit sheepish. "Errr. Do you have a copy of the, errr, copyright assignment." "Why, Tony?" "Because, errr, we can't find ours." Of course I had, because I am an anal filer of things, but I must admit I just said I would try and find ours. Sorry Tony, I think I made you sweat for a few days. But we never got our quid after all. I ultimately gave Tony a copy of the assignment, but the process then threw up that we hadn't assigned copyright of the individual symbols for the events. The franchisees for the merchandising had asked for the copyright documents as they signed contracts with the Games Committee. Of course there weren't any, because nobody had thought to do it. Again, lots of people working very hard in all quarters, but nobody on the team for the City had done this before.

Again I let Tony Hill sweat for a bit (sorry again Tony) and toyed (but not seriously) with saying nope, we'll sell copyright to the franchisees, but then I would have been run out of my City for good.

And a little time later I nearly was. I had a beer with Michael Taylor, the editor of Insider magazine. This was as our work on the Games branding was coming to an end. The 'mascot' for the Games had been unveiled. It was 'Mr. Blobby' with a Games logo on. My worst fears were realised – a global stage for my City and Mr. Blobby in office to represent us. As it turned out the Commonwealth Games blobby didn't actually figure, I don't think. At least I never saw him in action. Maybe everybody realised how bad he/it was.

I chatted to Michael about this and he asked me to write a story for Insider.

Or at least be interviewed for a story about it. I agreed, because I was stinging. I thought, I'll just get my point across and get it off my chest. Which I did, along with statistics about the demographic of the North West and how much we could have raised in merchandising by appealing to a broad age demographic, as opposed to Mr. Blobby only appealing to six to nine year olds etc., etc. I thought it was quite constructive, if a bit mischievous. The journalist asked if I had any of David's drawings, which of course I had and lent them to her.

I thought nothing more of it really, until a few weeks later we had our usual Friday after work beer planned at Revolution on Deansgate Locks, with the team we worked with from the Games office. Helen and I strolled over in the afternoon sunshine to meet them, said a cheery hello and suddenly noticed that the sunshine had turned to frost. Insider had used the Kit story as both its front cover and its main feature. And we hadn't seen it, although the Games office had. Ooops. I felt a bit like Nixon must have done when Watergate was exposed. Although all I had done was tell the truth. Insider had taken up the cause, because Michael amongst others could see it and I think the thrust was a little bit harder hitting than I had intended.

I don't think that I was ever flavour of the month after that, although in truth I never had been. Ah, well.

Eventually, in 2002 the launch event of the Games arrived. We went along, of course and I looked around me in wonder at the branding, the creativity and the scale of the whole event. It wasn't the Olympics, but it was close in every other aspect. The stats said later that it was broadcast to a billion people world-wide. So that's not bad. And as I walked away in the early hours of the morning I felt like I had been to a funeral. I thought that I would have felt elated, but just felt like I was walking away from burying a close friend.

The years 1988 to 2002 had been a 14-year project, with all the striving before that to get to this point. My 'ambition' as I left college in 1974. It all sounds great doesn't it?

Ambition (nearly realised), but it had been the proverbial roller-coaster, with the highs probably being equalled by the lows along the way. A funeral. Howard got a Knighthood, quite rightly.

I guess I never felt the same about work again. In truth it had been a slog for a few years. Maybe I stuck at it too long. At the end of the decade we had re-branded the business. Design and marketing was changing beyond recognition and the traditional skills I had learnt were no longer necessary to compete. I was far too long in the tooth after 25 years of running the business to adapt successfully (although in some aspects I am still producing good work to this day. But based on experience, not computers).

At that time we had employed a consultant to look at the business. He did a 'client interview' session, with some of the clients having been giving us business for a decade or more. One old, valued client said that we were 'like a pair of comfortable old slippers.' Now I am sure that this was meant well, but didn't go down well with me. My (our) reaction as a business was to re-brand, but on the basis of getting as far away as possible from being a comfy pair of old slippers.

We sat down and talked. I talked about the great brands and definitively Virgin had it. I am old enough to remember being shocked by the word. It was never, never used in day to day language, apart from in Church on a Sunday morning with 'Mary' attached to it. We talked about taboos, as Virgin as a word had been to use before its launch onto the world.

What taboos remained that could be used to shock, as Virgin had? Sex, creed, race? Race? Have a look in the Oxford Dictionary (sic): 'Race, a group of designers, like minded people.' There you have it. Perhaps 10 years too late to have avoided the comfy slippers, but a good, energetic, slightly risqué at times name. In 1999, Drawing Board ceased to exist and RACE came into being. Broadly the same people, but a new image. Problem was two years on and I'd just been to the funeral of a close relative. I was just short of fifty and too old a fart to rejuvenate myself as well as the business. About a year later the funeral and all sorts of other circumstances combined to make me realise that I had had enough. At least of exactly what I had been doing for the previous nearly 30 years. Somebody said to me you could be a consultant. Nah, I'm retiring. And so I told the clients, many of whom I had known for ever and some of them said, 'Don't blame you. But now you're retired can you do this project for us?' And so it was. I guess, as I have said, that I became a brand consultant.

Towards the end of the Games process I got a call out of the blue from Roger Stephenson. (OBE) He had been sitting on the Committee for MIPIM – Marche International de Professionel d'Immobilier - basically the biggest global property market in, well, the globe. It was and is held each year in Cannes, at the Palais. "Richard," he said, "It's a mess. We need a really good stand design, worthy of our City. And we just can't get it sorted. Can you have a go?"

Well I did, with a few subsequent chats with Rog. It came near to presentation time and I said that I thought we could do with a model of the stand to explain the concept. Rog, enthusiastic as ever, volunteered his services. He wanted things to be right, which is why he'd asked me to design it. Now I should have known, knowing Rog. The afternoon of the presentation to the Committee came, organised by Marketing Manchester who had and still have responsibility for the show. There was no sign of a model as the 3 o'clock meeting time approached. I went to Rog's office in despair and there he was, at 2.45 still making it. At 2.55 we both left in separate directions and at 3.00pm we both arrived from separate directions. I said hello to the members of the committee...and Rog. The model fell apart, of course. Even quick drying glue takes more than five minutes. I apologised and said that we had had trouble with our model maker. Rog in incognito revenge gave me a hard time about not using good model makers. But the concept was approved and we got the job. I did the project for the subsequent six or seven years, but was ultimately fired and the job given to Ben Kelly. Can't argue with that.

But it was a lovely job to do and the best thing was that I got to stay in Cannes for a week each year. At the time that everybody I knew from Manchester was there too. Perfect. Once the stand was built I had a lot of spare time and so, each year, had taken to driving up into the mountains above Cannes. The Var region. I loved it. After the funeral I took to thinking, I'd like to live out here and so spent the next couple of years looking for a place. But the looking became an obsession and I convinced myself that I needed a place out there. And finally I found one. The story has been featured in The Art Observer and rather than re-telling it all again, it's probably best – if you are interested – to have a look at those words.

Art lover finds the spirit of Picasso

There was a seminal moment at the start of the decade when Richard Morris ended a fitful but long search for Le Minotaur, the house in Provence where Pablo Picasso lived, worked and died. Richard tells the story. "I have had a lifelong interest in Picasso – I guess almost an obsession. This stems from my days at art-college and one of my own tutor's obsessions. I guess it's not really Picasso's work... I'd rather sit for hours in front of a Rothko than a Picasso...but the amazingly complex make-up of the man.

I remember distinctly the news broadcasts in 1973 when Picasso died and a shot of him sweeping down the drive of Le Minotaur many years before in his Hispano Suiza. I have no idea what that occasion had been, but all the news channels used the same shot in announcing the story of his death.

I worked in Cannes each year for a short time for several years and also visited that part of the world regularly on holiday with my family. And during those times I wandered around casually trying to find Le Minotaur. I also wandered around thinking increasingly that I would like to live in Var, I liked the sunshine, I liked the people and I liked having the spirit of Matisse and Cezanne and Bonnard and Monet and Renoir around me. And all the others! Then one day a final piece of detective work led me to that same driveway at Le Minotaur - overgrown, tangled and with grand iron gates which had been chained up since the great man died. I stood there and cried with emotion. The water lilies in MOMA, the Rothkos in Tate Modern, the sun shining into Mackintosh's garden room at Hill House. A handful of others had moved me to tears. Anyone who loves art and the context of art will understand that.

And so I started looking for a house in Var. Two long years and dozens of houses later I was ready to give up...until Anick, my estate agent friend out there, said, "Just one more to look at," three or four hours before my flight back to Manchester. Despite my protests Anick drove (in her French driving style) up the mountain to the village of Mons. We walked into a house in this mediaeval village that wasn't exactly derelict, but was far from cared for. As Anick explained, a large family had lived there from the early sixties. The five kids had one by one moved to Paris and when the father had died years before his ailing wife had been left with the legacy of a large rambling maison du village, five floors, three or four staircases and increasing disability. I wandered around quietly, instinctively feeling that this was the house I had been looking for. Provencale, real Provencale. A mess yes, but something we could do something with.

The deal was sealed when I walked out of the doors from the top bedroom onto a terrace with a view East to West of the slightly curved Mediterranean horizon. No idea how far away that horizon was, although glimpses of Corsica are to be had on the clearest of days and that is almost a hundred kilometres. I did know that Cannes and the coast which I could see were thirty-five kilometres away and the mountains and valleys in between – which we now have nicknamed 'Middle Earth' – provided the most breathtaking of views. Deal done, I guess!

The legal process was tortuous, but the one thing that kept me going was the documentation. The family I was buying from were called Bastard. Not BasTARD. It's not pronounced that way in France. And so every document had MORRIS/BASTARD firmly emblazoned in large letters on the front. Funny thing is, Anick speaks perfect English, but somehow never twigged how funny this all was. She'd phone me and say things like, "Richard, the Bastards have had the phone cut off."

Anyway we got there eventually. It took about eighteen months to clear everything out, put hot water in, a proper electricity supply in, a good cooker (essential!) and decorate, buy furniture and generally exorcise the ghosts of the Bastards. Although one of the family's kids have been in touch with me recently and are calling to visit their old house. I asked Michelle Bastard whether this would feel strange and she said that time moves on and they'd like to visit and so, of course, they will be welcome any time."

I asked Richard whether he became disheartened during the whole process and he said that the task took on gargantuan proportions at times, partly working in Manchester and managing a building project in Mons. There were times, he told me, that he had to fly to Nice and back to Manchester on the same day, twice a week. Easy Jet had a reduction in their income stream when the house was complete and he made friends with the cabin crew on the Liverpool Nice route, who couldn't quite figure out what was going on.

Although, he said, "A big part of the project was trying to preserve the knackered bits of the house which date back to the seventeenth century and before, whilst making it liveable for us as a family. I have done quite a lot of property work over the years and my instinct is always to gut somewhere and start anew. But when you've got a door that's at least three hundred years old and has huge, drafty gaps around it because it's just worn away, what do you do? I think I have a different answer to my own question during Winter time and Summer time!"

On an early foray to the villages, looking for a house, Richard drove past a gallery on the outskirts of a neighbouring village. He was with his old friend Trevor who had been accompanying him on some of the visits. As Richard says, "Trev and I were pottering along in a little hired Peugeot when we both went, 'Wooa. Elisabeth Frink.'" In the sculpture garden of a small, private gallery were three beautiful Elisabeth Frink heads standing large on podiums. In the Var light they were exceptionally beautiful. Richard and Trevor wandered in and the gallery owners, Tessa Peskett and Nigel Cox have since become good friends of Richard and his family.

"I think being able to stumble across Elisabeth Frink sculptures, in the sunlight, next to the road sums up what I love about art in Var. You just stumble across things that are so unexpected and when you don't just stumble across them they are in the small galleries in every village. The ceramics are beautiful, the glass work is beautiful – we even have a glass blower in Mons who has created all of our sconces and light fittings individually – and the drawing and painting is at times exceptional. Tessa herself is a fine and accomplished painter and I have bought several of her works. And when she's not painting she sits and plays the cello with the light flooding through the windows of her and Nige's house, next to the gallery. As Tess once said to me, "Sometimes we have to pinch ourselves!"

"So what other works have you bought for the Art Lover's House?"

"Well, I've taken some over there and bought some there. For example one of my tutors at college (not the Picasso man, another tutor!) gave me two plaster sculptures he'd done in the sixties. Sadly Trevor Lofthouse died about ten years ago now, but I think it is an honour that I have a home for such a fine gift that he gave to me decades ago.

I've bought three of Tessa's works, which I love. And do you know they are all so different and – as is the way – I didn't notice until after I bought them that each had a moon 'motif' in them. Weird. Maybe subliminally that's why I bought them. Others I've picked up in the Puces – which are the French Flea Markets – for next to nothing, one or two I've paid too much for in brocantes or galleries. But hey we've all done that!

They all have a story. There is another English artist in nearby Seillans called Paddy Lovely. He paints horses – pictures of them that is, not paints the horses themselves. Although Paddy likes a drink to say the least and was telling my wife Michelle and I a story a couple of years ago about spiking a horse with something or other to make it stop running around so that he could paint it. Anyway Paddy was the worse for wear, but not apparently as much as the horse when he got the quantities he spiked it with wrong. Sorry, rambling a bit there, but maybe only in Var...

But anyway I saw a horse head sculpture he had created out of a piece of driftwood in a local gallery and loved it. I thought it was a bit expensive at thirteen hundred euros, but also thought that if I caught Paddy in a (ahem!) good mood I might get a good reduction. 'Give me five hundred euros because I know you like it!' he slurred. Maybe only in Var...

I've also collected odds and sods of things that just interest me. I recently bought a cast iron 'gargoyle' dog in a street market. Got the guy down from a hundred and fifty euros to ninety, gave him the money and then he just smiled at me... I still don't know how a friend and I lifted it into the back of my car, the suspension survived and then we carried seventy-five kilos of cast iron up five floors to sit on the terrace. Anyway I love it and my kids have christened it 'rusty.' It still scares me when I go onto the terrace at night and catch a glimpse of it out of the corner of my eye!"

Richard has also shipped his library of art-books out there and hopes to sit down and read them some time in the future. Apparently he has been gathering these for thirty years and still hasn't made a lot of progress reading them. He says that the house is always full of his family, kids and friends and so a week of just chilling and reading is not really on the agenda yet. And of course there's scouring the galleries, craft markets and Puce's to fill time.

"And you rent the house out at any time during the year, don't you?"

"Yes. Friends and family have free run of the house when they want it, of course. But I have a French mortgage to pay and it all helps when I have paying visitors there! Although I am very selective (well, to a degree!) in whom we rent to. The house is an authentic Provencale village house and not a Provence holiday home, of which there are many. I didn't want a breeze-block pastiche house with a swimming pool, I wanted a real house with real history and atmosphere which we could enjoy with authentic enthusiasm. And somewhere to collect even more art than I do at home!

All of our visitors so far have been like-minded and rent the house for the same reasons – they love art and love to live for a week or so in a genuine private house in which they too can enjoy the works and books that are there - and make some discoveries of their own. It's an hour's drive to the coast and the major galleries where they can see the major works of great artists - and it's a stone's throw from, for example, one of my favourite spots. The terrace at l'Hotel des Deux Rocs in nearby Seillans, where Picasso used to sit and drink and exchange ideas with Max Ernst, who lived in the village.

I think that their spirits are there still!"

Just one more mention that the only thing that kept me going through the tortuous French legal process was that the family I was buying from were called Bastard... Our house in Mons is where I pursue my other passion, given to me by my tutors from College. I collect art. Not high flying art, but art which interests me. I have two sculptures there which my tutor Trevor Lofthouse gave to me. But maybe more valuable to me is the fact that Tony Forster and his wife Polly spent their last holiday together there, not long before he died. The house is there because of what Fozzie instilled in me.

In recent years I have seen my city start to become European. Twenty years of hard slog and creativity have changed it beyond recognition. It is still changing, of course and as I have chatted through things with an old friend of mine, Helen Thomas ('Hey, less of the old!'), she has said several times that we've all done our bit in one way or another. She's right. Some have done a lot, others have done what they do best to the best of their ability. But I am a Manc and proud of it. And I'm also proud of my City as it starts its next steps. After the Commonwealth Games, Michael Taylor and Insider asked me to write a feature: 'What next for Manchester?' I wrote about another vision, if that's not too poncy a word. That was that we and Liverpool evolved along the Manchester Ship Canal to become one great cosmopolitan entity. A bit like Los Angeles in structure I think, but with more substance. Maybe that will come true over the next century. I've been lucky enough to work with Peter Saville over the past three or four years. He said to me once that he was "trying to blur the edges between fine and applied art." We've done the hard slog, getting everything moving. Maybe now is the time to start looking in a more abstract way at how our great City – and maybe Liverpool – can become truly European and truly global. Stepping up to another level.

And my last grumpy old man words on technology. Of the digital kind. I know that it's a modern world and technology is an amazing thing. Just look at my iPhone. But it dominates everything and there is no room for real people talking to real people. I really do believe that we will learn to harness it for the good of all and in these several thousand words I have gone from not even having a telly to having one in my hand wherever in the world I am. A while ago my daughter sat at her computer for three hours 'talking' via the keyboard to her friend who lives five minutes down the road. "Why don't you just go to Beth's house and talk to her properly?" I asked. I was met with a blank, uncomprehending stare.

And another close friend of mine, ace photographer Jan Chlebik (co-founding member of our own 'Grumpy Old Man Club') said to me recently, "The world is full of verbal and visual diarrhoea. Twenty years ago if you went to the Taj Mahal you would see a thousand people staring at it in wonder. Nowadays you will see a thousand people pointing the camera end of mobile phones at it. And if you said to them, 'What did it look like, they'd say I don't know. I'll have a look at Facebook." A simple observation, but profound.

So there you have it. A Manc in Mons, which is where I like to say I live. Rue Pierre Porre, Mons. A tiny, mountain top Provencale village. It all sounds so simple now this little story, but of course it's been heartache and tears, along with the good times. I said as I started to write that I wouldn't change anything from the intro and I hope that I won't. I've missed out 90% of everything and therefore 90% of the people involved. In some cases that was on purpose, because it's better not to write some things down. In most cases it's because there just wasn't the space or the capacity to do so.

I was chatting to Helen Plumtree a short time ago – one of the many people who went through lots of this with me – and told her that I'd been doing some necessary Spring cleaning in my office in Manchester, which I still have. (Oh and by the way, I also still live in the City Region as well as in France.) I took out a box from the top shelf in the store-room which I hadn't seen for years. It was full of the old employment files. As I gradually and painstakingly shredded everything I realised – and this is what I told Helen – that although I remembered nearly all of the names, some of them I didn't have a clue who they were. I'd employed them, or somebody in the business had, and obviously worked with them. Just couldn't remember them. Must be my age.

Or maybe they were forgettable. Mind you, it works the other way too. I had a meeting recently with a growing marketing communications company in the North West. The woman who runs it was asking about my background. For some reason she asked if I had known Bob Sutton and I said yes. "I did my work placement at Drawing Board," she told me. She then said, "Did you work for Drawing Board?"

Yes, but was I worth it?

May 2010

For posterity and for my five kids.
I told you it had been complicated.

But things change.